Transformation may have its [text obscured by barcode] *not be overly complex. Cathy* [text obscured] *childlike heart, yet she spea*[ks to] *our souls with the depth of a mature mother in the faith. This book unveils principles to guide our sojourn toward Christlikeness. But even more so, it invites us to imbibe the ineffably gracious Father-love of God, who is the very wellspring of personal growth.*

Mark Sandford
Founder and Director, Elijah Rain Ministries,
Post Falls, Idaho, USA

Three words stand out for me from this insightful and well-written book. They are HOPE, TRANSFORMATION and BECOMING. Full of wisdom, personal testimony and spiritual insight that has the potential to help followers of Jesus of any age and stage move forward, Cathy shares her own walk with Jesus in ways that I am convinced God will use greatly to build His kingdom.

Brian Andrews
Senior Pastor, Broadmead Baptist Church 1987 – 2010

A wonderful book and a great introduction to some powerful Kingdom principles. I love how simple yet profound the chapters and sections are to digest. Cathy has made it possible for anyone to grasp these Biblical concepts through real-life struggles and experiences.
Kathie Fetveit, Co-Founder of H.E.L.P. International
(www.heretohelpintl.org)

This book is the fruit of Cathy's life journey and ministry and she offers insightful keys to help people move towards wholeness. She writes from her own Christian perspective, offering hope to all who are seeking inner healing or wish to be available to others on a pathway of transformation. Through the use of reflective questions at the end of each chapter, the reader is invited to deepen their own journey with God. Cathy's honest and engaging account has the capacity to energise the reader's own life story. This book could change your life!
Revd Brian Howden, Baptist Minister, Spiritual Accompanier and Former Tutor in Christian Spirituality

KINGDOM KEYS

HELPING YOU
LIVE LIFE
AS GOD
INTENDED

Wendy

There's always more...!

Blessings

Cathy W ♡

Copyright © 2023 Cathy Wheeler

The moral right of the author has been asserted.

Apart from any fair dealing for the purposes of research or private study, or criticism or review, as permitted under Copyright, Design and Patents Act 1998, this publication may only be reproduced, stored or transmitted, in any form or by any means, with prior permission in writing of the publishers, or in any case of the reprographic reproduction in accordance with the terms of licences issued by the Copyright Licensing Agency. Enquiries concerning reproduction outside these terms should be sent to the publishers.

PublishU Ltd

www.PublishU.com

Scripture taken from the Holy Bible, New King James Version,
© 1982 by Thomas Nelson, Inc.
All rights reserved.

Scripture from the Holy Bible, New International Version®, NIV®. Copyright © 1973, 1978, 1984, 2011 by Biblica, Inc.™ Used by permission of Zondervan. All rights reserved worldwide.

Scripture taken from the Holy Bible, New Living Translation, copyright ©1996, 2004, 2007
by Tyndale House Foundation. Used by permission of Tyndale House Publishers, Inc.,
Carol Stream, IL 60188. All rights reserved.

All rights of this publication are reserved.

Thank You

Over the years my life has been influenced, shaped and enriched by countless ministries and individuals who have imparted wisdom, teaching and life. I couldn't mention or even remember them all, but I am grateful.

Special thanks go to Phil and our three sons, Matt, Jonny and Dan. I've learnt so much from you and am proud of you all. Also to my sisters and wider family, and to all those who have been "fathers, mothers, brothers and sisters in Christ" to me.

Thank you to all the brave people who have allowed me to walk alongside you in your journey to wholeness; it has not always been easy, but it has been a privilege to see the Father's love at work in your lives.

Thanks to our Hearts Resounding Team, especially for your support and encouragement over the past few months of writing, as other things have been put on hold. Also to our friends in Elijah House, from whom I've learnt so much, and to our church family here at Broadmead.

Thank you to the brave friends who agreed to read through the manuscript and who have added generous comments and encouragement.

Also to my two wonderful guest editors, Adele Butterworth and Rick McKinniss. Without your challenges, corrections, suggestions, wisdom and insights this book would be far less readable and interesting!

Thank you to John Cartwright for the photograph.

And finally thank you to Matt Bird and the PublishU team, for helping me to turn what was a nice idea into reality.

Contents

Part 1: Five Keys For A Good Foundation

Key 1   Be Like A Child

Key 2   Through The Wardrobe

Key 3   Always Give Thanks

Key 4   Hold On To Hope

Key 5   Keep On Keeping On

Part 2: Five Keys To Help You Grow

Key 6   Transformation In Three Not-So-Easy Steps

Key 7   Let Go Of The Rope

Key 8   Sort Out The Planks

Key 9   What You Sow You Grow

Key 10 How To Dismantle The Obstacles

Part 3: Five Keys To The Father's Heart

Key 11 God Is Always Speaking

Key 12 Your Heart Has Ears

Key 13 Becoming Who I Am

Key 14 Are We There Yet?

Key 15 What Is In Your Bag?

CATHY WHEELER

Foreword

"Kingdom Keys" is a book forged out of a journey of discipleship and healing; and out of learning how to help others grow in faith and in heart-healing. It isn't theoretical musings or a theological treatise. It is, however, both grounded in Biblical truth and very practical in its approach. How does one advance toward deeper healing and in connection with God and others? "Kingdom Keys" addresses these important life questions by providing key insights and practices to unlock doors to healing, spiritual growth and connection.

Cathy Wheeler has written an eminently accessible guide for this journey that comes out of her own experiences as a follower of Jesus and her ministry of helping others along the way. I've had the privilege of watching this journey – both up close at times and from a distance. She's a woman of great courage, perseverance, honesty and integrity. I'm delighted that she's sharing her thoughtful and helpful reflections of her journey in life and ministry with the rest of the Body of Christ. If you're looking for keys to help you advance in your own healing journey, or in how to help others along the way, this book will serve you well as a practical and insightful guide. I heartily recommend it!

Rick McKinniss, Pastor Wellspring Church, CT, USA

CATHY WHEELER

Introduction

Where and what is the Kingdom of Heaven? What did Jesus mean when He told Peter, in Matthew 16:19, that He would give him the "keys of the Kingdom?" In this book we take a closer look at what Jesus said about the Kingdom and why we need keys, not just to enter, but to live there, to experience the peace and joy that Paul described in his letters (e.g. Rom 14:17; 1 Cor 4:20). Even if you've been a follower of Jesus for many years, you may find there are hidden keys that you haven't yet discovered or made use of.

Nowadays, there are many different types of keys. I might picture a typical metal door key, but for younger people, that may not be the first thing that springs to mind! We use keys of all shapes and sizes, including pieces of plastic to open some car doors. The word "key" has become a verb: something you do when you type numbers or letters into a computer. Keyboards offer us alphabets, numbers and symbols and the musical notes of a piano. One of my favourite keys is a "jar-key," which looks like a plastic spanner and is perfect for opening those pots that are impossible to get into unless you have really strong wrists (I no longer have to ask one of the men in my home for help!). Similarly, keys in God's Kingdom come in various forms and we need to know how and when to use them in different situations.

Many years ago I was a relief care worker in a children's home for children with special needs. On one occasion, because staff were short, I was asked to spend a day in a youth detention centre. This was very much out of my comfort zone, but my role was mainly to chat with a group of girls, accompany them to the music room or kitchen, and generally be present during the day, keeping an eye on one vulnerable girl at night.

When I arrived, I was given a huge bunch of keys on a belt, plus an alarm button. Perhaps that should have been reassuring, but I realised I might need to use it! There were doors everywhere. Each time we went to a different part of the building, I had to unlock doors and lock them again behind us. All of the rooms were secured, and there were heavy doors dividing different sections of the corridors. However, my large bunch of keys was a lot smaller than those carried by the regular members of staff. Why? Because I had neither the authority nor the experience to know how to respond in a crisis, and I could have become a target for anyone wishing to make a run for it! Thankfully, the day passed without any incidents, but it illustrates the way keys and authority work together.

When we choose to follow Jesus, we enter God's Kingdom using certain "keys" that He reveals to us. We experience the joy of being welcomed into His family; we are like little children, delighting in the love of the heavenly Father. As our assurance grows, He wants us to mature, to explore all that this new life brings. Keys give us access, authority, responsibility and protection: we need these in order to bring more of God's Kingdom into our own lives, and the lives of others.

Our world is broken and we don't have to look too far to see the effects of humanity's selfishness and greed. In the beginning, Adam and Eve held the keys. They had free access to God, walking and talking with Him every day in the garden with no fear or shame. They had authority over the birds and animals and were responsible for caring for the world's resources. As long as they did as God required they lived in safety. After the Fall, all of this was lost, and the keys were handed over to satan. God always had a plan to take them back, however, and through Jesus He restores what was lost. This doesn't happen all at once, but gradually we discover how we can live as overcomers.

Sometimes people ask why God doesn't just intervene and stop all the suffering. If He's really in control, what is He doing about it? We need to remember that, although Jesus defeated satan on the Cross and took back the keys of death and of this world, satan is still at work, trying to convince people that God doesn't care and that He has no power to set them free. The more we take back authority in our own lives, the more His new Kingdom increases on the earth. One day there will be an end to all the suffering. Until then, He wants to pull as many people as will come, into the Kingdom.

Sometimes we can feel stuck: we can't find a way through, nor can we go backwards. We may have discovered that certain "keys" work really well at times like these, such as praise or intercessory prayer, and getting through builds our confidence. Then we hit a wall and the things that worked before appear to have lost their power. This does not mean we've failed. Sometimes Father God has to override the keys we are holding in order to keep us safe, or for the safety of others. Or He may be inviting us to go deeper, stirring in us a desire to discover more of the keys that we haven't yet recognised or learned to use. In all things He wants us to grow up into Christ.

In this book I share with you some of the keys I have discovered, or that others have given me. I'm sure there are many more, some that you may already have on your belt. This is not a comprehensive guide, and there may be chapters you expected to find that are missing. However, whether you are feeling stuck or content with where you are right now, I hope this book will give you a hunger to discover more of the keys God has for you to live your life to the full, as an effective part of His Kingdom here on the earth.

KINGDOM KEYS

CATHY WHEELER

Part 1
Five Keys For A Good Foundation

"I write to you dear children, because your sins have been forgiven on account of His name... because you have known the Father."
(1 John 2: 12-13)

In the Kingdom of heaven we can learn how to help one another discover who we really are.

Key 1
Be Like A Child

There was once a princess who, at the age of two or three, was kidnapped from the garden of the palace in which she had known only love, safety and delight. Her parents searched for her for many years. They longed to see their beautiful child again. They grieved for her, but never gave up hoping that she would one day be returned to them.

Far away in another country that had been at war with the princess's homeland, the little girl had been passed on to an old woman with several children and grandchildren of her own. The kidnapper had hoped to demand a ransom for her return, but had become ill and died, and no one remembered where the child had come from. As she grew older she learned to cook, clean and sew and to avoid the blows that came when she was too slow, clumsy or sad. Any memories of her childhood faded quickly in this new reality. She hid them away in her heart and after a while she stopped looking at them. It was easier to forget and accept the life she now lived. She didn't ever feel that she belonged and always knew she was an outsider, but she had no idea why.

One day a group of soldiers was passing through the town. She was now about eleven years old and had been ordered to serve them with refreshments. The captain, who had spent years searching for the girl, saw at once the resemblance to her older sisters. He questioned the old woman and, satisfied that this was indeed the missing princess, he brought her home to the palace.

There was such great rejoicing, such a sounding of trumpets, such celebrations throughout the kingdom at her return! For the little girl however, overwhelmed by the unaccustomed attention and confused by the different way of life, it was extremely painful. She withdrew into herself and would often sneak down to the kitchens where she felt more at home among the servants. They however, like everyone else, would scold her. Her sisters would laugh at her fear of horses, her inability to ride, and her lack of what they called "poise." The servants would snigger when she picked up the wrong fork or spoon, or each time she opened her mouth to speak.

Belonging

Jesus said that we need to become like a little child to enter the Kingdom (Matthew 18:3). This is one of those large, heavy keys; it should help us to kneel, to be humble, to realise that we cannot do anything to earn our way in. Just like the girl in the story, we are welcomed because our Father has invited us, and we are His. It is where we belong, and it is His love that goes out to find us and bring us home. This key is one to treasure and hold on to, because sometimes we forget who we are.

If this was a fairy story or Disney film, it would most likely all end "happily ever after." In reality, the princess will need a great deal of help before she is stable and confident, sure of her identity. Hospitals and GP surgeries are full of people who struggle with anxiety and who sometimes end up in deep despair. The heart knows when something is missing, but most often does not know where to find it. Churches are also full of people who don't fully believe they are accepted and loved and who are hugely insecure about who they are.

What does this girl need? Someone loving, patient and understanding who can help her rediscover her true identity. She needs someone who could teach her what she has missed without making her feel foolish or less than she truly is; who could help her understand why she finds things difficult, so that she can have patience with herself. If that person could be found, then even though this difficult part of her life will forever be part of her experience, it will not define her. She will always see things differently from those who haven't been there; she may even become more compassionate as a result, but she wouldn't remain wounded and handicapped by her past. She would be able to live from her true identity, rather than always believing she is a fraud and an outsider.

Becoming

When a person decides to follow Jesus, when he or she makes that prayer of commitment and crosses over from death into life, it is as if he has come home. He knows in his heart that he belongs, that he is loved, forgiven and made new. However, just like the princess in the story, we need to realise that we bring baggage with us. Our spirit is reborn, but our soul (mind, will and emotions) will quickly fall back into the old ways of seeing, responding, believing. We may begin by feeling exhilarated, but then struggle when old friends or family laugh at us or point out that we are failing in just the same ways as before. The voices in our heads accuse us and too often the fire of new hope is gradually dampened until it has almost, or completely, died away.

If we understand that this is a normal part of the growing and becoming process, it will have less power to discourage us, and we will more easily see it as something to help us grow, rather than something we ought not to be struggling with. Why, having begun with simple childlike trust in God's goodness, do we feel under so much pressure to act as though we have it all together; that we are "successful" and have somehow "arrived" as Christians?

For the princess, so much depends on how others treat her. Her access to her parents has been restored, but does she really know she can go to them whenever she needs to? The unkind taunts of others may convince her not to bother; that the King and Queen would also laugh at her and scold her. As she grows up, if these issues are not resolved, she may learn to misuse the authority she will have one day, because unhealed hearts are not able to love freely. She may learn to withdraw, or to treat others unkindly.

In the Kingdom of heaven we can learn how to help one another discover who we really are. The Kingdom is made up of people who are family. Together we can help to fill in some of the gaps and make up for what has been missing. This isn't automatic, or something we should demand or expect, whether we are giving or receiving. As our confidence grows, we will sometimes be able to care for our own hearts, and figure things out just between

God and ourselves, but usually we will find that we need the help of others. These keys, when we take hold of them, are not so easily lost again.

We need to recognise that none of us have walked the same path on our journey to the Kingdom. It can be helpful if someone shares with you what they did when they felt stuck. On the other hand, it can be very discouraging if it doesn't work for you. We are so often looking for quick fixes, but things that take a long time to build usually last longer, and we appreciate them more.

Trusting

Jesus says we need to be childlike. This is not the same as being childish. A child trusts, and recognises that he or she needs help. There are times, even when we have been in the Kingdom for a long time, that we need to remind ourselves of this. He is God and we are His children.

In 1 John 2 we read that the job of the "child" (which includes adult Christians) is to know that he is forgiven and to know the Father. This is foundational and yet I often meet Christians who, even though they've been believers for years, still do not have this assurance. It can help sometimes to watch how children and a loving parent respond to one another and remind yourself that Father God loves you far more deeply than even the best parent.

Babies have physical needs — food, warmth, being cleaned up. They also have emotional needs. Even tiny babies search for the face of the parent, who is like a mirror for them, telling them who they are. How many babies and little ones are starved of this attention because of their parents' lack of communication, now that everyone seems joined to a little screen that comes out of his or her pocket? Parents teach us how to be a child and how to trust. David wrote, "You made me trust in You, even at my mother's breast."[1] When this happens, it becomes much easier to transfer that trust to a loving heavenly Father. But what about when there are gaps in our ability to trust?

Someone I know, who had been going through a time of great disappointment and difficulty, was finding it hard to connect with God, and was aware he was keeping God at arms-length. The family had recently had a baby and moved house, and his older child, aged two and a half, was struggling with all the disruptions in her young life. She would become overwhelmed by emotions that she couldn't regulate, sometimes withdrawing and other times punishing the parents by hitting out at them. When my friend recognised that he was doing the same thing, it really helped him to understand his daughter. He also realised that Father God's heart for him was even more full of love than his was for his child. In that healing moment his ability to trust and hope began to be restored. He also became more patient with her.

It can be difficult for us, as adults, to connect with God heart-to-heart, but creativity such as music, art and poetry can help. This song is one of the first that I wrote as a young Christian:

"I will enter in through the veil,

Clothed in robes of purest white.

Jesus You have cleansed me,

I can stand in the light,

And kneel at the throne of grace,

Look into Your face,

And rest in the arms

That hold me, and surround me, filling me with love."

God's love for us is never dependent on our actions. He is love and just as a baby needs to drink in love from the adult, we need to know we are loved by Him. It's only because of what Jesus has done that I can enter His Kingdom. It's only as I receive His unconditional love that I can begin to know that I am His child. He gives us the Kingdom: a gift that we need to receive as a child.[2]

Identity

Several years ago I was going through a difficult time and I was asking God what to do about some of the decisions I needed to make. Everything felt very heavy, almost overwhelming. I knew I needed to take a step back and ask God where He was and what I should do.

Sometimes God speaks to me when I am listening to Christian music, as I close my eyes and let my imagination speak (more about this in Chapter 12). On this occasion I pictured myself as a small child (That was how I was feeling!) climbing up to a large table where Jesus was at work, dealing with a huge pile of paperwork. He smiled and gave me a large piece of blank paper, just as you might give paper to a child who wants to "help" the grown up by doing some scribbling or colouring. On the paper He drew the outline of the letter C, and showed me how to write a C inside its borders. In this unfolding picture I understood that "C" stood for Cathy. After a while the child got down happily and went off to play with her toys.

I knew somehow that the papers He was working on were concerning me and my life. Jeremiah wrote, "I know the plans I have for you... to give you hope and a future."[3] Why was I pictured as a child? There are things that are my responsibility, for example, to trust Him, and to do as He asks, but He doesn't want me to take on what is not mine to carry. The "C" represents identity. It's my job to find out who I am, within the boundaries that He has set for me. This is not the same as the world's quest for self-fulfilment, a discovery of the person I would like to be or that others think I should be. Instead, He helps me to discover who I am in Him, the person He has called me to be. That is the place where I will find fulfilment, peace and rest. The journey there may be bumpy, but if I follow Him it will be good, because He is good.

Knowing my identity as a child of God is an important key and not one to leave at the front door once we are inside. We will need this many times going forward in our journey.

Application

How do I discover who God is calling me to be?

You may want to try the following exercise and then pray the prayer below.

On a sheet of paper draw the outline of the first letter of your name and, with a different pen, write the letter inside. You could vary this by writing your whole name, using your favourite colours, or decorating the letters with things that are special to you, but keep the decoration inside the borders.

Prayer:

Father God, this is me. I give You my heart, my hopes and my dreams. Thank You that You love me more than I could imagine. Help me to trust You on this journey of discovery. Help me find the keys I need as I try to live the life You have for me. Amen.

It is often in really difficult situations, when we cry out to God, that we discover He really is there and will help us.

Key 2
Through The Wardrobe

If you've read C.S. Lewis' "The Chronicles of Narnia" series or watched any of the screen versions, you'll remember that Lucy discovered Narnia when she fell out of the back of a wardrobe. Here was a parallel universe, full of talking animals, wonderful friends and terrible dangers. All that the Pevensie children learnt there, they were able to take with them into their "normal" life back in England. It gives us a picture of what it's like to live in this world and at the same time be citizens of the Kingdom of Heaven. We are somehow able to live in both places at once. We can learn to hold open our connection to the Kingdom with our heart, or spirit.

Churches don't always agree on how we should teach about the Holy Spirit and we sometimes avoid this subject in order not to cause controversy; there are opinions and views that can be polarising. I'll share a few things from my experience as I learnt how the Holy Spirit helps us and I will also share my understanding of what the Bible says about this important matter. I hope you will be able to apply what I've written to your own understanding of the work of the Holy Spirit.

Years ago, I was a member of the ministry team at a conference in London, where a well-known evangelist was speaking. When he gave an altar call, hundreds of people came forward to repent and ask for forgiveness so they could be saved. As the team was made up of people from many different churches and denominations, we'd been asked not to pray for anyone to be filled with the Holy Spirit. There are differing opinions on whether or how we should do this, so to avoid unnecessary disagreements, our role was simply to help people respond to the message of salvation.

A young girl came to me and told me she had repented several times before but had never felt forgiven, so she was sure she hadn't done it properly. It is the Holy Spirit who leads us to Jesus. When we realise we need forgiving and we confess and receive that forgiveness, then peace and assurance comes. It is the Holy Spirit, the Spirit of Truth, who witnesses with our spirit that we have become children of God.

Once I watched an experienced children's worker praying with a little girl who had just asked Jesus into her heart. When the lady asked her how she felt, she told us that her tummy was full of butterflies and she had a look of pure delight on her face. This was the Holy Spirit whispering His love to her in a way that she could feel, bringing her assurance that He was with her.

At the conference I hesitated, but only for a second. I asked the young woman if she had ever asked the Holy Spirit to come into her heart. She hadn't. I confess I did look around to check that no one was watching and then did what I'd done many times before. I told her she didn't need to keep repeating the prayer of salvation, but to ask for the Holy Spirit to fill her. Her face was beaming as she finally felt His presence, and she even began to speak in a new language of praise. She went away filled with joy because now, at last, she really knew in her heart that she was forgiven, and that she belonged to God's family. "The

Spirit Himself testifies with our spirit that we are God's children." (Romans 8:16)

Our team leader noticed her and commented, "She looks happy!" I didn't dare explain why, although I'm sure he would have been very pleased with what had happened! Had she already become a Christian? Was this the moment she got saved? Sometimes our need to put everything into neat theological boxes can get in the way of the relationship that God invites us to enjoy with Him. In any case, we need the Holy Spirit to help us. As our journey in the Kingdom continues, there can be specific obstacles that block us for which we may need different keys. He can help us to discover what they are.

Our Helper

As a new Christian I spent a gap year working in a children's home. I loved the children, but felt very inadequate and was afraid of most of the staff there. After a couple of weeks it was clear I was not doing well and I was ready to leave. Then, as I was reading a Christian book in my room, I experienced being filled with the Holy Spirit. For me it was like drinking a glass of wine, as warmth flowed through my whole body. Something happened that was tangible and real and it gave me confidence that I was not alone.

Other people noticed the difference. Within a couple of weeks I was given more responsibilities and at the end of the year received a glowing report. How did that happen? Only with the Holy Spirit's help.

Even so it was a very tough year, and I would get up each morning with a sick feeling of dread in my stomach. With early starts I didn't always manage to spend time with God first thing, but I remember that I always paused by the door before going out. I asked the Holy Spirit to fill me again, to breathe His breath into my heart afresh, and then I felt ready for what was ahead. Just as we put clothes on before going out, we need to clothe ourselves with Jesus if we are to stay tuned to God's heart.

It was good training for me. It is often in really difficult situations, when we cry out to God, that we discover He really is there and will help us. I found that when I was consciously keeping a line of communication open to Him, listening in case anything dropped into my spirit, He would give me wisdom, suggesting things I could do or say in the moment that I needed it. Sometimes the fear that drives us to our knees is the very thing that helps us to become strong, because we discover that He really will help us as He promises.

You Must Be Born Again

One of the most well-known verses in the New Testament is John 3:16, "For God so loved the world that He gave His one and only Son, that whoever believes in Him shall not perish but have eternal life." We usually think of belief as something we do with our heads. If we can see it, touch it or see it as logical, then we are prepared to trust it. If not, well, that is what faith is for, isn't it? But faith in God cannot be reduced to a mental assent to something we cannot grasp.

Sometimes when people talk about faith, they describe something separate from themselves; something you pull out when there is no logical argument to lean back on. People say, "I have my faith," as though it's an object and a place to put all their unanswered questions and doubts. It's the "get-out-of-jail-free" card to fall back on when there are no other ways to answer why they believe.

I have come to understand faith as actively trusting someone or something you are willing to depend upon. You trust because you know (or at least you are fairly certain and willing to take a risk); not because you don't know. Of course, you will never have all the answers and you will sometimes have huge doubts, but you trust a person, or in this case Jesus, Father God, the Holy Spirit or all three.

So how do we develop that kind of trust? And what did Jesus mean when He spoke about belief? This came in response to a question by Nicodemus. Jesus began by saying that we have to be born again to enter the Kingdom. This is a term we use quite freely nowadays, but to Nicodemus it must have sounded jarring and inexplicable. Jesus went on to explain that the Holy Spirit gives birth to our human spirits. We cannot enter the Kingdom without the Holy Spirit's help.

When we are born again, we know it in a deeper place than our minds. We know in our spirits that we belong and sometimes we sense His presence "like butterflies." This is the spirit-to-spirit connection that was lost after the Fall. Adam and Eve used to chat freely every day with God, with no shame or fear. Jesus had that same connection and He offers to restore that to us through the Holy Spirit.

Some people talk about the "God-shaped vacuum"[4] we all have in our hearts until we believe. We were created to know Him and to relate to Him with our spirits. The enemy will try to offer spiritual experiences that counterfeit God's love, but they never satisfy. Our spirits come to life when we are awakened to God and reconnected to Him. Now we can continually drink from this water of life. Paul wrote to the Ephesians saying, "be filled with the Spirit" (Ephesians 5:16). The Greek tense he used is present continuous, so that it literally means, "be being filled" or "go on being filled…"

Paul explains in 1 Corinthians 2:10-16 that the Holy Spirit helps us understand what God has given to us. He ends by saying that we have "the mind of Christ," but he means that this comes by revelation and not through logic or great brain power. When we enter the Kingdom, our spirits wake up and can connect with the Holy Spirit. He is our teacher and little by little, what we hear in our spirit filters through to our minds, and we have those light bulb moments when we suddenly know something is true, even if we can't explain why with our heads.

Different denominations might disagree on the work of the Holy Spirit today, but all agree that our God is three in one, and that Jesus promised to send the Holy Spirit after He ascended to heaven. The Holy Spirit is the third person of the three-in-one God, and the One who is our Teacher, Comforter and Guide. He reveals Jesus to us just as Jesus reveals the Father. Some streams emphasise the Word, some the Father's heart, and others, the work of the Holy Spirit. We need all these resources to demonstrate God's love and minister the life of the Kingdom.

Application

If you're not sure whether you've really entered the Kingdom, why not stop now and ask God? A simple prayer of confession and faith, such as the one below, can start you on a wonderful journey!

"Father God, thank You for sending Your Son Jesus to die in my place on the Cross. I confess that I've said, done and thought things that I need forgiveness for and I have left things undone that I should have done. Please forgive me.

"I receive Your forgiveness now, and I turn away from that way of thinking, believing and living. I choose to follow You Jesus, My Saviour and Lord. Please come and live in my heart today. Amen."

You can also ask Jesus to send His Holy Spirit to fill your heart and even if you have done this already, we all need to be filled again from time to time because we leak! You could pray the following prayer:

"Dear Holy Spirit, thank you for revealing more of Jesus to me. I need you to be my Teacher and my Guide. Please come and fill my heart (again) with Your living water. Amen."

If you are still struggling with doubt, or lack of assurance, there may be some obstacles that need removing. Do keep reading and ask God to show you what they are!

Giving thanks is a key that can release us when we are stuck, unlocking the hidden treasure we need to go forwards.

Key 3
Always Give Thanks

During my gap year I attended a church where a lady gave me a cassette tape full of worship songs. Do you remember those old chunky cassette players? You press "Open," slide the tape in and there are five buttons to push down along the front – "Open," "Go," "Stop," "Fast-Forward" and "Back." After that we graduated to CDs, MP3 players, and now, the wonders of wireless bluetooth technology!

But I loved that cassette player. I used it every day during my quiet time. It helped me to tune in to God's heart and it always lifted my spirit to be ready to face the day. Without realising it, I had become quite dependent on it. Then one day, disaster struck! The cassette player stopped working. I know that, for many of you, this may not seem much of a problem, but imagine if your mobile phone breaks, or the WiFi goes down and there's no way to reconnect. I had no mobile phone, no computer or laptop back then. There was only a red telephone box at the top of the hill. I was working in a strange town, in an emotionally draining job, and this was my lifeline! Also, on a volunteer's pocket money of £5 a week, I couldn't afford a new one.

As I cried out in desperation to God (sounds over dramatic I know, but it's how I felt!), I sensed a nudge to pick up the guitar lying in the corner of the room. In those days most Christian songs, or choruses, had three chords and were easy to play. I had even written out my favourites in a book, including "Trust and Obey," "What a Friend we have in Jesus" and several shorter ones taken straight from the Bible. These were great for getting truth into your heart and mind. However, although I knew a few chords, I'd never tried to play them myself.

Some of you may be thinking, "Yes, what a great idea, just play the guitar!" At the time it seemed to me to be nigh on impossible — as if I was being asked to push a heavy boulder up a hill. However, with no other option, I had a go and managed to work out the chords to most of the songs in my book. I discovered that singing with my guitar was way more effective in helping me connect with God than just listening, or quietly singing along with the cassette. It also lifted off that heavy feeling that seemed to envelope me at times. I was really surprised by this. Of course, God wasn't surprised. In fact, I think He set it up! It was like the difference between digital radio on FM and a scratchy signal from a foreign country.

Once my new routine was established, the tape player began to work again, and there was no reason for this other than perhaps an angel holding on to the tape before so it wouldn't go round! I didn't go back to the old routine after this. I had learnt something about the power of praise.

Why does God want us to give thanks and praise to Him? Is He insecure, in need of our adoration or wanting to remind us of how worthless we are in comparison? Not at all! He asks us to do the thing that He knows will bring us freedom, because He loves us. Giving thanks is a key that can release us when we are stuck, unlocking the hidden treasure we need to go forwards. Giving thanks reminds us that God is there, that He is for us and that we are not

God! We see the silver linings, the potential in ourselves and others, instead of mistakes and failures. We see the hope when all seems hopeless.

Is it just positive thinking or a kind of mind-over-matter exercise? It is true that optimism can help your mood, or mental state and it is tiring to be around people who are always negative and grumbling (or to be that person ourselves). However, there is far more that is happening when we worship than a mental exercise or a shift in mood.

The Psalmist explains in Psalm 100:4, that we enter God's house through gates of thanksgiving. Giving thanks moves us nearer to Him, away from what drags us down. When our thanks becomes praise, focusing on who God is rather than on what He has done, we draw nearer to Him, entering His courts. The next step is into the Holy Place, where we can be "lost in wonder, love and praise." Here in God's presence, we learn to receive His love and respond with adoration.

A Place of Springs

One of the better-known Psalms is Psalm 84 and several songs have been written to express the beauty it conveys. It begins, "How lovely is Your dwelling place" and goes on to describe the joy that we experience in God's presence; knowing we are loved and accepted by Him and experiencing the blessings of being in His family. The psalmist then describes a pilgrimage; a journey through the Valley of Baca. This is possibly an actual dry valley or it can be translated, "the Valley of Weeping" or "affliction."[5]

It's easy to thank God when things are going well, but what about when we experience pain, sorrow or fear? How should we respond when we don't understand what is happening, or how to change the situation?

Verse 6 reads, "As they pass through the valley of Baca, they make it a place of springs; the autumn rains also cover it with pools."

It's important to notice that they, the pilgrims themselves, are the ones who make it a place of springs. Then, the rain comes to soak the ground. When we, or others, are in a difficult place, we should, of course, pray that God will send the rain: the blessings that we need to turn our deserts into gardens. However, we have a resource within our own hearts that we can tap into. Jesus promised to give us a well of living water that would spring up inside us, bringing eternal life (John 4:13). He was speaking about the Holy Spirit, Who comes to live in our hearts when we become Christians.

In the Valley of Weeping we need to grieve and to lament. When we are able to share that with God and to invite Him into our pain, there is often a sweetness and comfort even in the deepest sorrow. From our tears will come springs that can bring new life in time.

When we are in a dry valley and everything is difficult, choosing to give thanks can be like trying to dig in stony ground. However, this can open up a well and release water stored up deep within our spirits. You may not even realise the water is there, but when we connect with the

Holy Spirit He fills us with life-giving water. We tap into a river that fills and refills our spirits and the flow gets stronger, pushing obstacles out of the way. Jesus went on to say that we need to worship "in spirit and in truth" (verse 24). The truth is there in the songs and hymns, or the prayers of thanks we use, even though what we feel may be telling us the opposite. When we express praise, even when everything in our body, mind and emotions is battling to do so, or perhaps especially at those times, we strengthen that connection. It's a bit like the exercises that athletes use to push their bodies to the limits. When they need that extra bit of strength for the race, it is there because they practised so many times.

Unconditional Love

Sometimes we're afraid to come to God because we've been holding on to some anger or resentment against Him. We feel we should sort that out first, but the best way to do that is to come as we are. He knows already anyway; it's no secret to Him! He will not reject us or turn us away on account of our imperfections. We can never be perfect! We need to know that His love for us is unconditional, because it's based on who He is, not on who we are.

Psalm 73:25 gives us an example of a man who was struggling with envy and resentment. Drawing near to God reminded him of God's love and goodness, as he declared, "Whom have I in heaven but You?" His emotions and attitudes changed as God remained steadfast, unchangeable; the perfect Father and a safe refuge for His people.

I once observed a small girl who was extremely tired after trying to keep up with some older children. They had all been running up and down a huge staircase in an old mansion, hired for a church weekend away. The girl's daddy called her and said it was time for bed, but she stamped her foot in anger and said, "No!" This was a little girl who was usually very quiet and obedient and I watched rather anxiously to see how her daddy would respond. Instead of scolding her, he scooped her up in his arms where she promptly burst into tears, burying herself in his embrace. It was such a good picture of the Father's heart for us. We want to go our own way, but as soon as we come to Him, He will hold us in His arms of love. Connection with Him can resolve any resentment we may hold in our hearts.

Am I Bothered?

At times we may resent having to give thanks and wonder why God doesn't just act anyway. I sometimes hear people say, "God is in control," not realising they are using it as an excuse for passivity. We need the childlike trust of Key 1, but as an active choice and not as a denial of responsibility.

Another statement that I often hear is, "God understands," when people know they should do something, but would really rather not. Again, we may argue that God has the power to change things so why do we have to do anything? We may be missing the amazing opportunity to partner with God in the battle to restore what has been lost and stolen from us, from our families and from our nations.

All Things?

On the other hand, we can sometimes use "truth" to encourage a friend who is struggling and end up heaping discouragement on him instead! This is when we inadvertently use Bible verses as weapons. We want to be encouraging, supportive and we suggest a verse that seems to "fit" the situation. One of the most quoted is Romans 8:28, appearing on coffee cups, place mats, posters and so on. It's a wonderful promise, but the version usually used states that "all things work together for good." It suggests that we should stop worrying and wait for God to do something. We should just give thanks and have faith in Him.

I have a problem with that! I do not believe that all things work together for good! That may shock some of you, but we need to remember that it wasn't written in English, and translators don't always get things right.

If "all things work together for good," what does that say to the person who has just experienced trauma or is going through grief? It sounds shallow, insensitive and hurtful. It suggests that what is happening is somehow a good thing and part of God's plan. We need to remember that the world is still under the influence of the evil one. People have freewill and make bad choices, which can then hurt others who are innocent bystanders. It is certainly not God's will that children are abused, that people are enslaved and that injustice occurs in so many ways because of man's selfishness and greed. This does not sound like Jesus to me.

The best teaching I've heard on this uses the NIV version, which reads, "In all things, God works for the good of those who love Him, who have been called according to His purpose."

I prefer the alternative version in my NIV Study Bible, which says, "God works together with those who love Him… to bring about what is good."

The most important thing is that it is God who works, not the things nor the situation. This is the promise: whatever is thrown at us — whether from the enemy, other people, our own foolish mistakes or simply because the world is broken — He is at work in these situations. Redemption is possible and He has a plan to turn things around. We are not alone, having to figure it out by ourselves.

The second point is that He is working with us.

If we don't get this part, we can tend to sit back and wait for God to make something happen. I often hear people say something like, "I don't know what God is playing at…" or "God promised but it hasn't happened."

God calls us to work with Him, to partner with Him and that is such a privilege. He is like the proud shop owner who can add to the sign above the window, "… and sons/daughters." We need to be asking what we can do; not simply waiting for Him.

Our purpose or calling is to seek His Kingdom first. Sometimes the good that results from it is for someone else. If our hearts are looking for the specific outcome that we want, we may be disappointed. God never promised that hardships won't come. In fact, just the opposite is true. The New Testament teaches us to expect hardship and trials.[6]

Application

1. Giving thanks and praise is something we can practice and build into our daily lives. It is most effective when we do it from our hearts. To help you with this, think about how you can best express your heart. You may want to sing, to read a Psalm or poem aloud. You could try illustrating your favourite Psalm or writing your own prayer of thanks. There are many art forms that can help you express your thanks to God.

2. Is there a situation in which you've found it difficult to keep praising God? Remember, you don't have to thank Him for the situation. Focus on His love for you. Try reading a Psalm out loud that reminds you of His love, such as Psalm 139. Then read a joyful psalm of praise such as Psalm 150.

3. This week, try to think of one thing every day that you can give thanks for and write it down in a journal.

4. Try writing your own psalm or poem to God. Begin with a verse of thanks, then write a verse of praise that describes who God is. The final verse is worship in which you express your love for Him.

> *Godly hope brings assurance and peace; it is a confident expectation of good.*

Key 4
Hold On To Hope

My husband and I enjoy watching "Saving Lives at Sea": a TV documentary series showing the work of the lifeboat volunteers around the coast of our country. They are amazing in their selfless efforts to rescue people who, for various reasons, have become stranded, injured or washed out to sea. We are shown real footage of dramatic rescues and have been moved to watch them find more than one person who has been adrift for hours on a tiny inflatable, surfboard or damaged boat, clinging on to the hope that someone will come.

We have an inbuilt desire to survive. If no one comes, at some point that flicker of hope is extinguished and, like the tragic moment in "Titanic" when Jack lets go of the float, we become lost or overwhelmed.

Where does hope come from? It is not listed by Paul as one of the gifts or fruit of the Spirit. Paul writes that the Holy Spirit is the Spirit of hope, and that He fills our hearts with hope. The hope He gives us is different from what the word is usually used to describe. For example, "I hope I pass my exam," "I hope it doesn't rain today," "I hope the washing machine doesn't break." These are all examples of wishing for a good outcome but fearing that it won't happen. This kind of hope may be based on statistics or past experience, but it's very different from what the Bible calls hope.

Godly hope brings assurance and peace; it is a confident expectation of good. "May the God of hope fill you with all joy and peace as you trust in Him, so that you may overflow with hope by the power of the Holy Spirit" (Rom 15:13). Like love, hope is a characteristic of God and He wants to share it with us. If we have no hope, it's something we can ask Him to give us. We don't have to manufacture it ourselves by trying harder to believe.

A Fortress of Hope

Once when I was going through a very difficult time, a friend pointed me to Zechariah 9:11-12, which is now one of my favourite passages from the Bible. "Return to your fortress, oh prisoners of hope," it says.

It's an unusual expression, to be a prisoner of hope. However, when you consider that God or Jesus Himself is the God of hope, then we can read it as saying that we need to return to Him, to allow Him to captivate our hearts again, to surrender to Him. He is inviting us to be His prisoner and this is a good thing. It's always helpful to look at a verse in context. Here, Zechariah is sharing God's promise to people who have lost a great deal. He tells them, "I will restore twice as much to you."

I clung to this verse and began to picture what a fortress holding a prisoner of hope would look like. If I am in a prison of fear, every way I look, I see what makes me afraid. I may be catastrophising or remembering what went wrong before. There may be really good reasons for me to fear. This isn't just a question of being a "glass-half-empty" kind of person. The enemy of our souls wants to bring us into fear and doubt, so that we will stop trusting what God has said or believing that He is faithful to His promises.

Wouldn't it be better to be imprisoned by hope, so that every way you look, you see things through a lens of hope? This is what I began to do. Instead of fearing the worst, I chose to believe that God really did love me and that He had a plan to get me through to a place of safety and healing. As I began to look through the lens of hope, everything looked different. Sometimes I would recognise a specific fear that didn't line up with God's Word. At those times, I would choose to let go of it and believe what God said instead. This was challenging on the days when the voice of fear seemed overwhelming. However, as I persevered in choosing to believe God's truth rather than trusting what felt true at that moment, the balance began to shift.

Psalm 91 helped me to personalise God's promises. Sometimes I would read it aloud, replacing "you" and "your," with "me" and "my" or using my name. For example, verse 4 becomes, "He will cover me with His feathers, and under His wings I will find refuge." I would read it slowly, a few verses at a time, picturing the fortress and the feathers that cover me.

Hope and Fear

It is not wrong to fear, although I used to think so. I believed that giving in to fear was "falling short" and that I needed to repent, but this brought me into deeper guilt and shame rather than freedom. As a young Christian, I heard some teaching on fear and I was set free from a totally illogical fear of moths. I discovered that this fear had been rooted in a particular episode of Dr Who, a popular children's TV series, in which giant moths were chasing the doctor and his friends! Butterflies were OK, but if I was trapped in a room with a moth, panic set in and I had to make an exit! Can Jesus free us from these kinds of irrational fears? Absolutely!

This was different from the unbalanced teaching I heard later. I was with a few friends and we listed and prayed against many different fears that we were aware of. When nothing seemed to change, we were disappointed and added more fears to the list, getting ever more specific. We were focusing on the problem instead of the solution. We knew the verse that says, "perfect love drives out fear" and that if we fear, we are not yet made perfect in love (1 John 4:18). We read it as a condemnation, but really it is an invitation. Jesus Himself is perfect Love, the One who can send away the fear. Freedom from fear is possible if we will keep searching for His perfect love.

Job and Hope

I decided to look at "hope" in the Bible. This is a great way to learn what the Bible says on a given topic or word. Take a concordance and look up every time that word is mentioned and write it down. Look at the context to give yourself an understanding of how the word is being used.

I was amazed to discover how often the word hope is used in the Book of Job. It was not what I was expecting. Job is possibly one of the last places I would have expected to find this word. His situation was apparently so very lacking in hope throughout most of the book.

However, I found myself identifying with Job in a way I hadn't before. Just like him, I wanted to know why certain things that had happened to me had been allowed by God and what God thought about it. Was I guilty of some sin that deserved His anger, meted out by the circumstances I had experienced? Like Job, I did not think so, but I needed to hear from God. I knew what some people thought, but they didn't all agree, so it was difficult to trust anyone's opinion, including my own. With Job I cried out to God and I recognised that I had been carrying a lot of shame that did not belong to me. I realised that deep down I sensed there had been an injustice, but I didn't have the words or understanding to explain why.

In the end God didn't answer my question, just as He did not answer Job's. Instead, I had a revelation that brought me great peace. I realised that I had felt abandoned by Father God. When Jesus took my place on the Cross, He also experienced abandonment. I had always unconsciously believed that if God abandons you, it must be your fault; you must have deserved it. You had to figure out what you needed to be forgiven for in order to get back to a place of peace. Does that sound familiar? This is what Job's friends were telling him, but he was indignant, because he knew deep down that he had done nothing to deserve the catastrophic losses he experienced.

Suddenly, I recognised that, although Jesus cried out to God, "Why have you forsaken me?" Father God had not forsaken Him at all. It felt true, but it wasn't. God had a plan all along to rescue Him. And for the first time I could believe that this was true for me also. Although some very difficult things had happened, it did not mean that God didn't love me, nor that He did not have a plan to rescue me all along.

It was a deep and profoundly healing time for me. Hope was restored after months of turmoil, depression, doubt and wanting to give up. I was not yet where I needed to be, but I was certainly once again on the way.

Hope is, of course, bound up with love and faith. Our hope needs to be focused on our Father's love for us. Childlike trust, gratitude and connecting with the Holy Spirit are all helpful in this. If our hope is in a specific outcome or in a particular answer to prayer, we may be disappointed. These can get in the way when God has a different plan. If our hope is in Him — in His Kingdom — we will keep looking through the lens of hope, the walls of the fortress that protects us from fear, whatever may come our way.

Application

1. Take some time to have a conversation with God about hope. What are you hoping for? Is it based in truth or in fear?
2. Ask God to show you if there are hopes you are holding on to that get in the way of the hope He wants to give you.
3. Ask Him to fill your heart with His hope.
4. Use the words of the song below to express your desire to put your hope in God today:

1. I have put my hope in You,

Oh Lord, for You are faithful;

What You've promised You will do,

And Your love will never fail.

So I will wait for You,

When I think I can't go on;

When my strength is gone,

I will lift my voice in praise,

My hope and my song.

2. Like a river that's run dry,

Is my heart without You;

How I need Your love again,

Like a life-giving stream.

So I will wait for You... etc.

You have been my fortress and my shield;

You've captured me with hope instead of fear.

My hope is in You all day long,

My Lord and my God,

My hope and my song.

Oh, I'm running again to my fortress,

Oh, I'm running again to You.

Oh, I'm running again to my fortress,

Oh, I'm running again to You,

My hope and my song.

KINGDOM KEYS

It is in a trial that we find out what we're made of.

Key 5
Keep On Keeping On

In this section, we're looking at foundational keys and recognising that we begin our new lives as Christians like little children. Children need to know they are loved and we want to protect them. However, we also want them to learn how to recover from life's knocks. A grown man or woman who still runs to mother when hurt or upset is not a great picture!

My husband Phil has always liked growing things and a few years ago we signed up for an allotment not far from where we live. After experimenting with potatoes, tomatoes and various kinds of vegetables (some more successful than others), we decided to try looking after chickens. There was already a chicken house on the plot and we prepared it for its new residents. We chose four: Henrietta, Holly, Hazel and Harriet – one black, one white and two brown. They can be very entertaining and have given us plenty of eggs over the past couple of years.

At first, the eggs were very small, and occasionally we found one without a shell. There was a wet patch of straw, and what looked like a piece of paper, but was in fact the egg membrane. What the egg lacked was the outer layer; the chickens needed to eat more grit in order to produce the firm, protective shell. The white and yolk are the treasure, the food that contains and brings life. With no protection this can be trodden on and wasted.

As I thought about this later, I saw that what we have in our hearts when we come to know Jesus is treasure. If we don't know how to protect it, it can be trampled on and lost, and we won't be able to share it with others. I sensed that to build resilience, like the chickens, we need to develop more grit.

I also thought about the old practice of collecting birds' eggs, sucking out what was in them and keeping the shell as a trophy. Perhaps some of the rituals we hold on to can become like this – empty shells that once held life and truth. We may not even be aware that the life has gone out of them. We cannot feed or sustain others with empty religion. On the other hand, any truth we have to share needs to be well-defined; able to withstand knocks and bad weather.

How Do We Build Resilience?

Once when I had taken my toddler to a playground, we heard a commotion from the other side of the park. A little boy, aged four or five, had fallen from a swing and was clearly hurt. We watched as he ran to his mother, yelling loudly. She opened her arms to him, but before she could hug him, his father grabbed him and smacked him hard, shouting at him for making such a fuss. The boy quickly stifled his sobs and set off for the swing again.

This was hard to watch, but the father probably thought he was helping his son to be resilient and not like a baby. Perhaps he was embarrassed by the crying, but I wondered what effect it had on the child's heart. He stopped crying and for the father this would have been a good result. However, it is likely that the shell around his little heart grew tougher, leaving less room for the treasure inside to grow.

So many children, especially boys, have been told that "big boys (and girls) don't cry." No one wants to encourage attention-seeking behaviour, but how do we get the balance right so that real pain can be comforted, helping children to keep their hearts open, rather than to shut down?

We cannot protect our children from pain, and it does no good wrapping them in cotton wool, avoiding places where they may tumble, or face rejection or failure. If they don't experience pain as children, how will they know what to do when it comes later in life? However, we can be there to offer comfort and to assure them that, even when they fail, they are still amazing and loved. They will learn that there will be comfort for the painful times.

This is the kind of heavenly Father we have. If we, like this little boy, did not experience comfort as children, we may find it hard to go to Him when we are hurting; but He is there with open arms to welcome us. If we have been over-protected as children, we may wonder why God doesn't rescue us from difficult situations when we call to Him. We may question His love when times are hard. We need to understand that sometimes this is how He helps us to grow spiritual "muscles" — resilience for what may lie ahead — which will help us to keep going when things get tough.

Setting Goals

When he was younger, our eldest son often found it difficult to finish things, especially if they were not particularly interesting to him or if he got stuck (I have his permission to tell this story). Instead of finding a way through, he would put them off until later, sometimes forgetting about them until he ran out of time and the deadline was passed.

One day he, his dad and a friend decided to cycle the almost nine hundred miles from Land's End to John O'Groats to raise money for charity. The first part of the journey was extremely hilly and waiting for bike repairs slowed them down. It also rained every day, but they were not put off. Even when Matt's knees became really sore, needing support bandages, he didn't give up. After two weeks of determined effort, they all made it and were able to give generously to their charity.

This built something into our son. He realised he could push through difficulties, ignoring the pain, knowing that the final achievement would be worth all the hard work. Since then, he has found it easier to complete those tasks that, in the past, he would have left undone.

Doing the hard stuff is important and we can help our young people, and our own hearts, by setting practical goals that are tough but achievable.

Perseverance

When we look from the top of a mountain or hill at the valley below, it can be easy to see the route we need to follow. Later, perhaps struggling through brambles and boggy ditches, meeting barbed wire fences with no gates, we might start to question whether we are on the right path at all and to consider turning back and starting again.

My husband loves to find alternative routes back from the path we set out on when we are walking. On one occasion, after scrambling through bushes and crossing a muddy stream, we ended up in someone's garden, with two huge dogs running towards us! We prayed hard, of course, and were very glad when someone (we're sure they didn't see us) called them away, so that we could make a run for the road ahead. He thought it was hilarious, whilst I was struggling to "count it pure joy"!

It is in a trial that we find out what we're made of. People watching reality TV shows such as "I'm a Celebrity…" are eager to see whether the participants will hold their nerve or crumble when faced with all kinds of scary beasties. The audience often choose the people they dislike the most or who scream the loudest, to take on the so called "trials." We might imagine ourselves in their situation and think that we would cope better, but what about when things don't go according to plan in our lives?

Don't Let The Fire Go Out

Have you ever felt that you have been falsely accused or that your motives have been misunderstood? It's important at such times to ask God to search our hearts, and if possible, talk things over with honest and wise friends. We can all be tempted to think too much of our own ideas. However, sometimes God asks us to do something, knowing that it will be opposed, because He wants us to grow more resilient.

We might assume we heard incorrectly and give in all too quickly, especially when leaders disagree with us. However, if it really was God, our hearts will know that He ignited a passion that we have allowed to be extinguished. When this happened once to me, I spent several weeks wrestling with guilt and depression, sure that I had let God down, but powerless to do much about it.

Around that time I heard a message by Melinda Fish and it changed everything. She explained that we shouldn't be surprised when we meet opposition. The people most likely to discourage any new move of God are other Christians who don't understand what you are doing. For good motives, they will try to protect what they know and understand. However, if God has asked us to do something, "We must not let the fire go out, because a King has lit it."

As hope returned, I found a new determination to fight for what I believed God had shown me. This was very unlike my usual timid approach, but I discovered there was courage hidden in my heart. I knew I had to do it His way, respecting and honouring the views of others and that I may still be misunderstood. I wrote a letter, explaining our vision in detail. This time the door opened.

What did I learn from this? Sometimes God leads us to a pathway on which we're likely to hit a few fences, boggy areas or even get chased by dogs! He knows it will be difficult, but that is not the test of whether or not we should go ahead. How we respond can make us stronger if we learn to do so His way. I had always relied on being "nice," hoping that people would understand my motives and believe what I said. Suddenly I hit a wall and had to change tactics or give up. I had to learn to find my voice and fight for what God had shown me, and to figure out what I really believed about it.

I could have assumed, when things were not going well, that I had been wrong. Of course I did question what I had heard, but hitting a road block doesn't necessarily mean we heard incorrectly in the first place. It may be that God is inviting us to dig deeper; to find an inner resolve we did not know was there.

However, demanding to be heard or doing things in an ungodly way is not the right way forward. Phil and I did not knowingly trespass on someone else's land; it was only when we saw the dogs that we realised our mistake! If we're careful to operate with the character described as "the fruit of the spirit," especially with patience, kindness, gentleness and self-control, then obstacles can become opportunities for growth as we learn to build relationships rather than tear them down.

Application

1. Is there a situation in your life where you seem to have been blocked from going forwards?

    Which fruit of the spirit do you think you may need to help you keep going?

2. Have you been falsely accused of something?

    Did this stop you from doing something you believed was God's plan for your life?

3. Take some time to talk with God about these things.

KINGDOM KEYS

CATHY WHEELER

Part 2
Five Keys To Help You Grow

"I am writing to you, young men, because you are strong, and the Word of God lives in you, and you have overcome the evil one."
(1 John 2:14)

> **When we recognise and face up to our responsibility, when we are moved with compassion and long to act differently, not only out of fear or shame, but out of love, then our repentance will bring lasting change.**

Key 6
Transformation In Three Not-So-Easy Steps

In this section, we look at some of the keys that help us to mature, to become "overcomers" and our first key is repentance. It may surprise you that forgiveness and repentance do not come earlier in the book. After all, our new life begins with forgiveness, and Jesus' first message, according to Matthew, was "repent!" However, there's much more to discover about both keys as we grow.

I sometimes think of forgiveness and repentance as "master keys." If you're not sure how to respond in any situation, ask God what you need to repent of and/or who you need to forgive. There may be other, more specific keys that we could use, but these two can get you a long way! We will look at forgiveness in the next chapter.

Confess Or Repent?

The word "repent" can seem heavy, because we associate it with judgement and guilt. We repent when we begin to follow Jesus, confessing or admitting things we've done wrong and God forgives us. After this first step, we usually think of confession when we need forgiveness, but many still struggle to believe that they are forgiven. As we consider why this might be, we will look more closely at these two words.

Most of us know this promise, "If we confess our sins, He is faithful and just and will forgive us our sins and purify us from all unrighteousness" (1 John 1:9). If we still feel guilty, we may try "standing on the Word," declaring that we're forgiven, proclaiming promises and declarations about our new lives in Christ. But what if the doubt is still there? Is it lack of faith or could it be something else?

The word "confess," meaning to admit sin, occurs only five times in the New Testament, whereas "repent" or "repentance" occurs fifty-four times! Luke states that repentance brings forgiveness, "Repentance for the forgiveness of sins will be preached in His name" (Luke 24:47). So do these two words mean the same thing? Although they are often used interchangeably, recognising the difference can help us experience the assurance of God's forgiveness.

Repentance is not the same as confession; we need both. To confess ("homologeo" in Greek) is "to agree with" or "to say along with" God. Our confession always needs to be made with a repentant heart, otherwise we're like the child who is scolded and forced to say "sorry," when he isn't sorry at all! God loves us so much that, when we confess, He will go on forgiving us, even when we do the same things over and over again. However, He wants us to know that repentance is also a wonderful gift. Without it, we remain like little children splashing in the shallows; never learning how to swim.

Repentance is choosing to take up my cross daily, dying to my own way. When I confess, I agree with God and admit something. When I repent, I change something, or at least, I am willing to change. Should I do this in my own strength? Sometimes. And sometimes only God can change us.

In the Bible, there are three words that have been translated "repent." Each word corresponds with a step we can take as we learn to overcome through repentance.

Step 1: Choosing To Change

The first word is the Hebrew "sub" or "shuv"[7] which means "turn back, turn to, return, bring back, restore, be recovered."[8]

This was the message of John the Baptist at the beginning of the New Testament:

"Repent, for the Kingdom of Heaven is near" (Matthew 3:2).

John was calling people to turn back to God and said they should produce "fruit" or evidence, in the form of changed behaviour. He baptised people with water, signifying that their wrongdoings were forgiven and they were washed clean.

This is how we usually describe repentance, picturing a one hundred and eighty degree change of direction. When we first decide to follow Jesus, giving up our way for His, when we recognise a destructive behaviour pattern and replace it with something better, we have basic repentance: Step 1. It's not always easy, and can involve a tremendous struggle, but it will be worth it. We find that we're forgiven, washed clean and we can make a fresh start.

We could say that Step 1 repentance occurs mainly in the soul.[9] I recognise, with my mind and emotions, that something needs to change, I apply my will to bring that about and I choose better actions. This can bring huge benefits, both to ourselves and to others, as we learn how to follow God's ways instead of our own.

Repentance is not just turning "from" something, but "to" something, or rather to God. When we turn to Him instead of relying on our own resources, we find help to develop healthy relationships with one another and, where possible, to restore what was broken. When we choose His way, we discover it's much better than ours!

However, when the change we hope for doesn't come, it can be tempting to blame others or to assume that God just wants us to be happy. We may settle for the way things are, not realising there is more; we may come under condemnation and question whether we are really forgiven and loved by God. If we're struggling to produce "good fruit," we need to know there is a Step 2.

Step 2: Change From The Inside Out

"Nacham" is the second Hebrew word for repent. It means to "relent, repent, change one's mind, be grieved; to comfort, console, express sympathy; to be comforted, be consoled."[10]

This word best describes the repentance taught by Jesus. He began His ministry with the same words that John used: "Repent, for the Kingdom of Heaven is near" (Matthew 4:17).

Then He added something: "Repent and believe the good news" (Mark 1:14).

Whereas John brought a warning, Jesus brought hope. When Jesus was baptised, the Father declared from heaven, "This is My Son whom I love." This was the good news! The God that people knew only as a holy Judge was the Father of love. This required a huge shift in their understanding and is something He wants us to know for ourselves.

What do we learn about repentance from Jesus, the One who did not need to repent? In Biblical culture, unlike our western thinking, "belief" is not something that happens primarily in the mind. What we believe in our hearts, in the core of our being, will supersede what we think we know in our heads.[11] For example, you might know that spiders are harmless, but if your heart believes they are scary, logic may fly out of the window whenever you meet one! Jesus is not inviting us to mentally grasp that we are loved by God. He wants us to know it deep inside, making it easier to resist doubts. How can we know something in our hearts, even when our head has questions?

In Acts 19:1-6 we read about a group who had been baptised with John's baptism. They had repented and received forgiveness, but Paul explained that they needed something more: to be baptised into the name of Jesus. If you take on someone's name, as in adoption, you become part of the family. When we are baptised as followers of Jesus, we are adopted as sons and daughters and our hearts are made new. The Holy Spirit comes into our hearts and everything changes (Romans 8:15-16).

Even so, without an understanding of "nacham" repentance, we can remain stuck at Step 1. "Nacham" means more than just changing direction. It includes a sense of compassion, grief and comfort, impacting us at heart level. In the Old Testament it usually describes God relenting out of love and compassion,[12] but in two significant places it refers to a person.

Jeremiah

First, Jeremiah describes "nacham" repentance:

"After I strayed, I (Ephraim) repented; after I came to understand, I beat my breast. I was ashamed and humiliated..." (Jeremiah 31:19)

This repentance results from deep grief and shame and clearly the word "sub" was not sufficient.

Sometimes, when a person has confessed something they have done, we can be too quick to assure them that they are forgiven. Have they really understood how they have hurt other people and God's heart? It is not kindness to avoid confrontation when it is needed. God's kindness leads us to repent, not just to confess.[13] He knows that we need to feel shame at the pain we have caused before we can experience the power of His forgiveness. We need to be humbled by the recognition of our own weakness, frailty and capacity to fail. Then, when we repent from this deeper place, the comfort we receive from God goes to the depths of our hearts and we are transformed from the inside; not just outwardly.

In Step 2 there is humility, godly sorrow, and a desire to change, not simply to be forgiven. We repent, not only of our actions, but also of the motives and desires hidden in our hearts. Covering up any ugliness by trying harder doesn't work. It will keep rearing its head until we are willing to repent and to be changed on the inside.

Making Amends

There are times when, besides repenting, we need to make amends. This is not often taught in churches, although 12-step programmes recognise how important this can be for restoration and healing. Sometimes we confuse God's grace with allowing people to get away with wrongdoing, as long as they express an apology. Even worse, it's then up to the wounded person to offer forgiveness, otherwise he or she may be perceived as "unchristian."

When our repentance is shallow, it reveals immaturity or fear. The immature do not cope well with correction, but want things back to "normal." They may apologise, even demand that forgiveness be extended and act as if everything is fine again. We may unwittingly encourage this if we major on forgiveness and forget to protect and heal the wounded (see Jeremiah 6:14). Making amends helps us to take seriously the pain we have caused and think carefully before doing it again. This may include standing down for a time from any leadership role, being accountable to others and getting healing for ourselves, so that trust can be rebuilt.

With Step 2 repentance, we understand how we've hurt others and we long to do whatever is needed to bring restoration. There is humility and a sweetness in the pain, because we know that God will show us the way through to redemption. If we're still making excuses, blaming others or covering up what we've done, then making amends in some way can help to soften our hearts enough for us to take Step 2.

Job

Secondly, Job used the word "nacham" after his encounter with God. His friends were convinced that the disasters he experienced were a punishment and they urged him to repent ("sub"), but Job insisted that he had done nothing wrong (Job 34:33). He was correct in this. However, after meeting God, he did repent (Job 42:6). Job used the word "nacham," although the difference is not apparent in our English translations. This was a heart-level repentance, expressing a wealth of emotions: grief, shame and humility at his own presumption and the darkness in his heart, but also wonder, awe and comfort at hearing God's voice. God didn't even answer his question, but he no longer needed an answer. After his repentance, healing and restoration came.

As Paul said, "Godly sorrow brings repentance that leads to salvation and leaves no regret, but worldly sorrow brings death" (2 Corinthians 7:10).

Like John's disciples, Jesus' followers are baptised in water, but washing away past sins is only the beginning. Jesus' baptism[14] purifies the heart with fire, and the temptation to go on doing wrong is dealt with, not by our strength of will, but as God changes us on the inside. Some of these changes are instant, but more often there is a process of recognition, repentance and transformation, bringing an increasing assurance of the Father's love.

"Nacham" repentance can give us authority over things we have struggled with in the past. The Holy Spirit guides us as we continue to discover areas in our hearts that may need addressing. The more we know God's Word and understand His ways, the more we will grow. This brings us to the third step, and to Paul.

Step 3: Continue To Be Changed

"Metanoia" is the Greek word used for "repent" in the New Testament. It means "to repent, to change one's mind."[15]

At first glance we might think this is a translation of "sub," but Paul also understood belief to be something that began in the heart, not the head (see Romans 10: 9-10). We could therefore say that repentance, "metanoia" means "changing the way you think in your heart." Repentance that begins in the heart is "nacham" repentance.

Paul clearly expects believers to go on repenting, and being changed, because transformation is not a one-off event.

For example: "Or do you show contempt for the riches of His kindness, forbearance and patience, not realising that

God's kindness is intended to lead you to repentance?" (Romans 2:4)

Through repentance, we are transformed ("metamorphoo"). In Romans 12:2, Paul says that this occurs as our minds are renewed.

"Do not conform any longer to the pattern of this world but be transformed by the renewing of your mind."

We could conclude that change comes as we understand more of God's Word and alter our behaviour. Whilst this is of course important, transformation is not achieved through our own efforts. We get our word "metamorphosis" from this same root. Imagine how difficult it would be for a tadpole or caterpillar to change itself through sheer willpower! Real change begins in the heart and Paul is clearly talking about Step 2 repentance, or "nacham."[16]

In another letter he explains that we need the Holy Spirit's help for this ongoing transformation to take place, "We are being transformed into His likeness with ever increasing glory, which comes from the Lord, who is the Spirit" (2 Corinthians 3:18).

Or again in Philippians, "Continue to work out your salvation with fear and trembling, for it is God who works in you to will and to act in order to fulfil His good purpose" (Philippians 2:12-13).

The transformation that God intends is just as remarkable as that of the frog (although usually less outwardly dramatic!). It isn't something that we can achieve through willpower, nor does it come through God's power alone. When we recognise and face up to our responsibility, when we are moved with compassion and long to act differently, not only out of fear or shame, but out of love, then our repentance will bring lasting change.

Power To Change

In Step 1 we tend to focus on outward behaviour. We may try to justify our actions or we may condemn ourselves as failures. With only our own understanding and willpower, we can be in denial or become overwhelmed with guilt and shame. In Step 3, as the Holy Spirit brings conviction, we discover forgiveness, freedom from guilt and the power to change. Transformation comes as we live a lifestyle of repentance.

I remember going through times when I was sure that I had failed God. I would list all the things I needed to confess, asking for His forgiveness. However, I didn't feel forgiven; I felt worse! Then I learnt that conviction is the Holy Spirit's job, so I asked Him to show me what I needed to confess. I was surprised to find that His list was always much shorter than mine! Like David, in Psalm 139, I asked God to search my heart. Whatever He revealed was always mixed with gentleness and hope, as He assured me of His love for me.

Satan loves to accuse us, heaping guilt on us; after all that is his job! The Holy Spirit brings conviction in a way that makes us feel held. He does not condemn, but often gently points to something, showing us a way forward. There may be deep grief, but there is always redemption in His conviction. If He shows you something, explaining, or making excuses will not deal with it. The answer is to confess, ask for forgiveness and repent.

Ongoing repentance is not limited to mistakes, failures and so on. As God "prunes" us, the Holy Spirit reveals motives for actions that may appear good on the surface but are driven by other factors such as a need to be liked, to be perfect, a fear of failure or rejection and so on. Dealing with these hidden drivers frees us to love with a purer heart and the good is replaced with something better.

Praying It Through

At times we may need to confess to someone else before we feel forgiven but remember that confession is not repentance. I often find that when I lead people in prayer and ask them to repent, they struggle to use the word. They may skirt round it uncomfortably. They may use confess, sorry, and so on. They may even begin to declare that God has forgiven them.

A friend recently told me that praying through these things can seem like saying words and nothing is happening. Later however, the difference is amazing, and you suddenly realise that something has changed deep inside your heart! The prayers are not magic: we are agreeing with God and doing what He has taught us. This puts keys into our hands, keys that unlock prisons and set prisoners free.

If God has shown you something you need to repent of, there's a sample prayer below to help you. We need to be specific, rather than repenting of "all the things I ever said or did" and so on. Praying aloud helps you know your will is in agreement. I encourage you to practise that now, even if it feels strange!

If you sense a need to make amends, ask God for wisdom and perhaps share it with a wise counsellor. We can cause more harm if our motives are focused on our own desire for forgiveness, rather than the needs of the person we have injured!

Application

Prayer:

Father God, I recognise that I've been going my own way, but now I want to choose Yours.

Please search my heart and show me how I have hurt You and others, through my thoughts, words, actions or through what I have not done.

(Take time to wait and see what comes to mind.)

Father, I confess _____ .

Thank You that through the death of Jesus I can be forgiven and cleansed through His blood.

Thank You for forgiving me. I receive Your forgiveness. Please wash me clean.

Father, I now repent of _____ .

Thank You that through the resurrection of Jesus I have new life.

Please change my heart. Bring me to the place of deep repentance and help me to become more like Jesus. Amen.

KINGDOM KEYS

> **Forgiveness is a key that sets me free from a prison of bitterness, resentment, self-pity (never our friend) and self-justification.**

Key 7
Let Go Of The Rope

Our second "master key" is forgiveness. I first discovered its power during my gap year, when I was volunteering with children with special needs. The other volunteers complained about the headmaster and I soon found out why! On a cold, wet morning I was working in the garden with a group of children, weeding the flower beds. I had no idea which plants were weeds, but thankfully one of the girls was happy to show me. Finally, we all trooped inside, grateful for the warmth and the smell of lunch. Our relief was short-lived, however. The headmaster angrily ordered us all back outside for another hour before we could eat because he was not satisfied with our work.

The children were cross, but they were used to this. I had not expected to be treated as a child even though, to be fair, I was still a teenager. It was hard not to be indignant; I wasn't sure I had signed up as a gardener anyway!

Later, praying in my room, I sensed God was asking me to forgive this man. A knot of resentment and anger was growing inside me as I explained why this was unfair, and why he did not deserve it, but the impression persisted. In the end, I reluctantly agreed. It took enormous willpower, but the fruit was amazing! Suddenly all the stress was gone and I felt so much lighter. I looked out of the window and the rain, still falling, now refracted the sun's rays, producing a rainbow. I knew in my heart that God was affirming my choice.

The others couldn't understand why I refused to join them in grumbling, but I knew resentment was not my friend. Forgiveness set me free, whether or not the headmaster ever recognised that he had been forgiven.

Having crossed that hurdle, I tried always to forgive quickly. Of course, God didn't always send a rainbow! He often encourages new steps of faith, but it is as we persevere in this new direction, even when the encouragement is not there, that we become stronger. It can be incredibly difficult at times but making a decision in your heart to live a life of forgiveness becomes a great weapon in your hand.

Sometimes the people closest to us are the hardest to forgive, but this is how our peace is restored. Forgiveness is a key that sets me free from a prison of bitterness, resentment, self-pity (never our friend) and self-justification. These all lead us deeper into the Kingdom of self. Forgiveness gives us a way back to the Kingdom of Heaven, which is a much better place to live!

Matthew and Forgiveness

Forgiveness is not passively sweeping things under the carpet and acting as though nothing is wrong. Nor does it mean we shouldn't go to the authorities when laws are broken. A good place to find teaching on forgiveness is Matthew 18. It begins with an invitation to trust, as little children, the Father who will leave the ninety-nine to go and search for one who is missing.

Then, we read that our Father is angry with those who hurt us and that they will face justice. From verse fifteen we read what can appear to be random statements, often quoted in other contexts, but I believe they belong together and they all teach us something about forgiveness.

What Is So Important About Forgiveness?

When Jesus taught His disciples to pray, He emphasised forgiveness (Matthew 6:9-13). He said that if we don't forgive, we cannot be forgiven. Then, in the Parable of the Unforgiving Servant (Matthew 18), He said that anyone who refuses to forgive will end up in prison. This seems unfair when we're the ones who have been wronged! In reality, there is nothing fair about forgiveness; it's only possible because of the Cross. Forgiveness is always a gift we don't deserve but refusing to forgive others brings consequences.

Supposing a daughter, let's call her "Sylvia," resents her mother's explosive anger, and vows never to treat her own children that way. Fast forward several years, and Sylvia is a calm, patient and organised mother of four. One day, one thing after another goes wrong, and she "loses it," yelling and screaming at her stunned children.

Order is quickly restored, but Sylvia has a problem. She has crossed an invisible line and cannot forgive herself. Because she has never forgiven her mother, she has no grace for herself. Now she is the bad-tempered mother she always hated as a child. Although Jesus paid the price for both mothers, she cannot receive that gift because she has closed a door and hardened her heart.

If Sylvia can forgive, she will experience compassion and recognise that we are all capable of failure. She will be able to forgive herself and receive God's forgiveness. That is her only way back across the invisible line. Otherwise, she may become worse than her mother, because now she sees herself as a monster, with no way to return.

What About Grace?

God loves us more than we can imagine, but love can ask us to do difficult things. Sometimes people say, "God understands" when they feel unable to forgive, expecting God to "let them off the hook" but this is a misunderstanding of grace. Grace gives us the strength to do things God's way. Otherwise, it's as if someone throws paint across our windscreen and all we see is the other person's failings. We refuse to wipe it off, but until we do so, we won't see clearly enough to move forward. We may even end up in a ditch.

Similarly, forgiving others is not the same as understanding or excusing them. If I forgive her, "because I understand why she did it," I'm excusing, not forgiving. Understanding can help, but God asks us to forgive whether we understand or not; whether she meant it or not. Grace gives me the power to forgive as God's love flows through me.

Dealing With Offences

Does this mean I have to stay and continue to be hurt over and over again? In some cultures, even parts of the church, women especially have been expected to keep quiet and "submit" to ill-treatment. This is not what Jesus is saying and forgiveness does not mean being a "doormat."

In Matthew 18:15-17, Jesus gives practical guidelines on how to respond when someone offends you.

I wonder how often we actually follow these! When did you last go and tell someone she hurt you or take along a friend if she didn't listen? Isn't it easier to avoid her and perhaps talk about her instead? Acting as though everything is fine won't resolve anything. The next step is to tell the church, which is not an invitation to gossip! Someone in leadership may help to resolve things. When necessary, he may decide to alert everyone and put safeguarding measures in place.

Finally, treating the person as a "tax collector" doesn't mean throwing them out. We should forgive, but we don't have to trust everyone. When "tax collectors" truly repent, they can be welcomed, but we should exercise wisdom, using boundaries to keep ourselves and others safe.

Keys To Bind And Loose

In the next verse, Jesus repeats His promise to Peter from chapter sixteen,

"I will give you the keys of the Kingdom of Heaven; whatever you bind on earth will be bound in heaven, and whatever you loose on earth will be loosed in heaven" (Matthew 18:18).

If someone has offended me, it's as if an invisible cord binds us together. Whenever I see him or am reminded of him, the cord is tugged and unwelcome thoughts, feelings and conversations surface. They might leak out, but usually they get pushed down, ready for next time. Even if we forget the offence, those cords can remain. Our "buttons" get pushed and we overreact, sometimes without knowing why. When we forgive, we "loose" ourselves from these invisible ties.

This verse is often used in spiritual warfare prayer, but it also applies to forgiveness. We only have authority when we are under authority. My earthly choices (to forgive or not) will affect how well I am aligned with heaven, and unforgiveness may block the flow of heaven's life and blessings to and through me.

I was once attending a conference, knowing that forgiveness would come up, so I made sure I had forgiven everyone I could think of before going! Even so, when we asked God to show us who we needed to forgive, six names came to mind. I was sure I had forgiven them, but as we prayed, emotions began to well up. I had forgiven with my mind, without involving my feelings. At last, I could give the buried pain to God and forgive from my heart. I hadn't realised the pain was there, but the peace and healing that took its place was tangible and real.

Sometimes we hide our pain because we feel guilty. We want to get rid of our (justified) anger and we stuff it back inside, not realising it's better to let it all out! Some of the Psalms can help us express deep, powerful and even ugly emotions. I remember repenting of anger, but never feeling forgiven. Finally, instead of asking God to forgive me, I poured my heart out to Him, expressing my anger and pain. Then, He gently asked if I was ready to forgive and I was! The pain went, along with the guilt.

The Importance Of Unity

During His last teaching before the Cross, Jesus prayed for the unity of His people (John 17). Unity can be a powerful motive to forgive, especially when we feel let down or betrayed by someone we trusted. Equally, if we realise we've hurt someone, we should take the initiative to go and put things right (Matthew 5:23-24).

We often use the next two verses to encourage ourselves when only two or three turn up for a meeting, but they also relate to forgiveness,

"... if two of you on earth agree about anything they ask for, it will be done... For where two or three gather in My name, there am I with them" (Matthew 18:19-20).

We declare this promise, as though speaking it makes it true, but we should not treat God's Word like a formula. We focus on the numbers, but He asks us to agree, to meet in His name as His representatives. How can we agree when there is unforgiveness? How can we represent Jesus if we can't hear Him?

Jesus lives in each of us, and we hear Him through one another. If I have not forgiven you, I will probably not hear

Jesus through you. Grudges block us from hearing His voice and become the "elephant in the room" that no one talks about. Others will sense the tension, even if they don't know the reason for it. Instead of flowing from heart to heart, spirit to spirit, the meeting becomes laboured as everyone tries to think of something to say, or else we go along well-rehearsed tracks that lack the life-bringing light that comes in when the Holy Spirit flows through each of us.

His promise is to be with us when we are in unity. We have to get rid of the "elephants." This doesn't mean we have to be perfect (we are all "jars of clay" and imperfect carriers of His love). The more we forgive, the more we will see and hear Him through each other, and the more His Kingdom will come.

Unlimited Forgiveness

Peter has been listening carefully and now suggests something he probably thinks sounds impressive: forgiving a person seven times. Jesus replies that our forgiveness should have no limit. Sometimes we forgive several times for a single offence, wrestling with it over a long period of time, as we gradually recognise how we and others have been impacted, until we are finally ready to let it go.

Forgiving From The Heart

Jesus then tells the story of the unforgiving servant (verses 21-35) thrown into prison after being forgiven a huge debt, because he refused to forgive a fellow servant. In the final verse, Jesus says we will be in that prison unless we forgive "from the heart." This phrase is so important, but what does it mean and how do we do it?

We think of the heart as the home of love and other powerful emotions such as compassion, grief, jealousy and hatred. To forgive from the heart is to feel and release our emotions; it is forgiving from the place of pain, where the hurt is lodged. Unfortunately, we often train our children to bury their emotions by demanding that they apologise, or accept an apology, without first helping them express how they feel. As a result, we learn that forgiveness is primarily a choice, or a decision, divorced from emotion.

How can we change this pattern and learn to forgive with both our mind and our heart?

Several years ago I was deeply impacted by teaching on forgiving from the heart by a pastor friend, Rick McKinniss. With his permission I've shared his illustration in many different settings and do so again here. Our previous pastor dubbed this "the McKinniss rope trick" and while it isn't magic, it is awesome!

Letting Go Of The Rope

I remember the first time I demonstrated this with a blue climbing rope and two volunteers — let's call them Harry and Pete! I represented Jesus, Harry pretended he had been hurt by Pete and they each held one end of the rope, the cord that bound them together.

Pete walked to the back of the room, and dramatically fell down, pretending to die. Offenders may move away or die, but our resentment still ties us to them. Looking towards Pete reminded Harry of his pain. I asked him to turn and look at me (or Jesus) instead and give me the rope, along with all his hurt, anger and resentment. Suddenly, Harry really got it. I can still see the look in his eyes of amazed relief, as he realised he could finally forgive the person in real life, who had caused him so much stress and pain. He wouldn't have to face him; he could do the heart work with Jesus.

Now Jesus can pour healing and comfort into our hearts. This is a Divine Exchange. He carries away my sin (anger, resentment and unforgiveness) and my pain, and in exchange I receive comfort, peace and hope.

The other person isn't "off the hook," because now, Jesus holds the rope. Situations can change when we no longer react in the old ways, and there is also a spiritual dynamic at work. I know of more than one person who has forgiven, without ever contacting the offender, who has suddenly received an apology or a blessing from him or her.

When I forgive from the heart, it's between me and God — a "vertical exchange." It is as if I am owed a large sum of money and I hand the unpaid bill to my Father, trusting Him to collect it on my behalf. I may never see the money, but I can trust Him with it because He is just.

Reconciliation

Reconciliation, restoring the "horizontal" relationship, is the next step. This is what we usually think of as forgiveness, but this is so difficult to do without first dealing with what is in my heart. If I forgive from the heart, reconciliation becomes much easier. I recommend working through forgiveness before attempting to reconcile. Otherwise, however much we try to hide any resentment, the other person is likely to be defensive and may retaliate.

Sometimes reconciliation is unwise and unsafe. We need to be careful not to retraumatise wounded individuals by insisting they reconcile with others who are not safe for them. This is especially true of survivors of abuse of any kind.

However, suggesting that a survivor doesn't need to forgive is unhelpful. It's forgiveness that releases them from the influence of the abuser, however long and difficult a journey this may be.

I once described the rope illustration at a meeting where some survivors had shared their painful experiences in churches. They were told they were at fault when they found it impossible to forgive. The example gave them hope, because they are not being asked to pardon or to face anyone. Instead, Jesus invites us to release our pain and bitterness to Him so that we can unhook ourselves from those who hurt us. When forgiveness is impossible, He will accomplish it in us, if we are willing.

If you, or someone you love, need help in this area, try to get someone experienced to walk with you through the healing journey. If you use the sample prayers at the end of this chapter, I recommend beginning with something small.

Some Points To Notice

- Did you know that "forgive and forget" is not in the Bible? When God "forgets" our sins, He no longer holds them against us. This does not mean He literally forgets! If we forget without forgiving from the heart, we've only put the offence out of our minds; our hearts still remember.

- We often say "that's OK" when someone hurts us, but it's not OK. Try saying "I forgive you," instead. It can sound awkward but keep practising! It validates your pain and may make the other person think twice before doing it again.

- The other person may never say sorry, and I don't have to wait for an apology before I forgive.

- There is a time for godly anger, empowering us to take action against injustice, such as when Jesus emptied the Temple. This anger is different from resentment or bitterness; it seems to flow through us cleanly, and does not leave a bitter taste, or lead us into self-pity.

Gethsemane

The way to the Cross is always through Gethsemane. Just as Jesus wrestled in prayer before being ready to submit to the Cross, we may need to wrestle with our deep heart's response. If you are struggling to forgive, don't give up. You may need time to comprehend what is in your heart and gradually release it to God.

Sometimes we need to forgive God. Of course, He hasn't done anything wrong, but I may be holding resentment against Him. Our minds might protest, but sometimes in speaking this out, people discover their hearts are angry at God. Forgiving God is releasing Him from my expectation that He will behave the way I expect Him to. It is honestly admitting I have judged Him. Try praying it aloud and see what happens!

I also need to forgive myself. Pride says that Jesus' sacrifice was not enough to deal with my sin; only everyone else's. If I insist on feeling guilty and punishing myself, I may be helping the enemy. Don't be tricked into straying into his camp but take the key and step back into Kingdom territory where you belong!

Application

Take some time to be quiet with God, inviting Him to show you anyone you need to forgive and why. Don't forget to include yourself and God!

Be specific. As you name feelings, it may help to picture putting them into a sack, or a wheelbarrow and leaving them at the foot of the Cross.

Don't rush this prayer. Ask God what He wants to give you to fill the empty space left in the garden of your heart now that the rubbish has gone.

Prayer:

Father God, who do I need to forgive?

Show me what I need to forgive him for and what got buried in my heart.

Imagine you are sitting next to Jesus and the person who hurt you is across the room. It can be so hard to look at her and the thought of forgiving her brings up huge, conflicting emotions. Now turn away and look into Jesus' eyes. Take hold of the imaginary cord that ties you to her and offer it to Him. As you do so, use the words below to tell Him what happened, and how you felt. Allow the pain to surface, put it into His hands, and let go.

Jesus, I choose to forgive _____ for _____ .

It made me feel _____ .

Jesus, I give You those feelings (anger, hurt, resentment, etc.).

I release (name) _____ to You and give You my end of the rope.

In exchange I receive _____ .

Take some time to rest in God's presence and drink in His love and peace.

Jesus is saying we need to be careful how we judge others.

Key 8
Sort Out The Planks

I once wrote two Bible studies for our Christian Union — one on forgiveness and the other on judgement, entitled "Judge Not..." I tried never to judge anyone and to be quick to forgive, always looking for the positives in others. However, there may have been some imbalance in my understanding; I have come to realise that there is a right way to judge and, in some situations, it's really important to know how to do so.

Judge Not...

Jesus said, "Do not judge or you too will be judged" (Matthew 7:1). He went on to say that if we judge others, we will be judged in the same way using the same measuring rod or yardstick. This is not a threat; He is explaining how things work.

The story of "Sylvia" in the last chapter illustrates this well. She judged her mother as a bad-tempered failure. Now, after acting in the same way, she attaches this label to herself. The more she tries to be different, the harder it will be. Without some kind of intervention, her children will undoubtedly judge her too and so the cycle will continue.

No one likes to be told, "You are just like your mother (or father)," unless it's a compliment! Yet how many parents realise they've become like their parents with their own children? Have you ever criticised or laughed at someone, only to catch yourself later doing the same thing?

Some would call this "karma," because there's a law written into God's universe that we reap what we sow (more on this in the next chapter). If you are struggling to overcome something, ask God whether you've ever judged someone else who acted this way.[17]

Jesus is saying we need to be careful how we judge others. When we label someone, declaring them to be the bad thing they did, we are sitting in the judgement seat that belongs only to God.

I once prayed with a man who had struggled to recover from the loss of his wife. Grieving is important, but sometimes we can get stuck there, unable to move on. I discovered that his father had been a strict disciplinarian and was often absent when he was a child, leaving him with an unhealed wound of abandonment.

The loss of his wife triggered this deep childhood pain and once again he felt abandoned.

After forgiving his father and repenting of judging him, he was able to release his wife into the arms of Jesus and to receive the comfort he needed deep inside his heart.

Then I wondered whether he had become like the person he judged. His children may have been staying strong for his sake, so I asked how they were coping. He told me they were fine; they didn't seem to have been affected very much.

I thought this unlikely and suggested he may have become like his father: not physically, but emotionally absent. He got it. Now he repented and made a commitment to be the father his children needed and to help them face and process their grief.

We do not always become like the person we judge but there will be a consequence of some kind. For example, if I judge someone in authority to be unfair, I may come to fear or resent everyone in authority.

When I first started learning French, none of us liked our teacher and we judged him to be a horrible man. He once accused me of cheating because I got all my homework right: I hadn't, I just tried hard because I was scared of him! For years afterwards I had a mental block when it came to spelling the word "exercise." I had misspelled it a couple of times and he wrote it with red ink in block capitals, followed by several exclamation marks, as though he was shouting at me!

Years later, after forgiving him and letting go of my judgements, I could see there was more to him as a person. He was an excellent teacher and I got good results, for which I am grateful. I also no longer have a problem with that word!

We also often make snap judgements, sometimes based on first impressions and past experiences. We once took a rhubarb plant to our son's house and, as it was getting late, placed it in the back garden. It was in a black plastic bag and was the size of a large cat, with leaves sticking up like huge ears. As it grew darker, Frida the dog began leaping up and down at the window, barking ferociously at this suspected intruder in her garden that, for some reason, didn't run away. She was also afraid. Jonny had to put her on the lead and coax her outside for a closer examination before she would calm down!

How often do we make up our minds about someone based on appearance or our first encounter, without being willing to take a closer look? Perhaps we could ask God to take us by the hand and show us how He sees each person, made in His image and loved by Him; we could give one another room to find our place and grow a bit before we jump to conclusions.

Does this mean we should never judge anyone or is there a right way to do it?

Judge Rightly...

We should, of course, judge between right and wrong, between what is and is not acceptable behaviour. This is different from judging motives or labelling people as the bad thing they have done. For example, a child may be tempted to steal from a sweet shop. If handled well, this could be an opportunity to help the child learn the difference between right and wrong. Appropriate consequences, such as being asked to pay for the sweets and apologise, should be accompanied by the child being welcomed back and reassured of her place in the family.

It's important to understand why she took the sweets. Was she hungry? Was it to prove something to her friends? Addressing insecurities is often the key to helping children choose better behaviour. If she is labelled as a thief, however, she may lose hope and respond by becoming even more adept at stealing.

When we judge out of love for the person, we are helping him to grow. Paul gives an example of this in 1 Corinthians 5, when he urges the church to judge a man who has been sleeping with his stepmother and expel him. Paul's judgement is rooted in love for this young man, as well as a desire to protect the church. He hopes he will come to his senses, remember who he is and return to the Father like the prodigal son.

Again in chapter six he says they should settle disputes by judging between one another rather than by going to court. This is not a suggestion that they should take the law into their own hands, as some groups have, covering up offences to protect their reputations. On the contrary, he expects higher standards and accountability from people who are learning to do things God's way. He is reminding them of who they are, and that it's not about winning their case, but doing it God's way. They, of all people, should know the difference between right and wrong, and yet they were asking outsiders to judge between them.

Paul's concern was to guard the church's standing before the world, but not in a way that would cover up abuses and wrongdoing. Setting boundaries and holding each other accountable helps everyone feel safe. Sometimes we are too quick to forgive, not addressing harmful behaviour and the pain it causes. However, Paul is not saying we should write people off, give up on them or reject them forever.

Paul also says that he doesn't care how anyone judges him apart from God Himself (1 Corinthians 4:3-5). Is he being arrogant in this? Actually, this is wise advice for us all, especially when we feel judged by others! Only God can truly see a person's heart and motives and we should be more concerned about God's opinion of us than about what others think. God loves us, far more than we can imagine. We are His sons and daughters and we must be careful how we judge one another.

Specks and Planks

In Matthew 7, Jesus goes on to say we might notice a little speck of sawdust in a brother's eye. However, because of the "plank" in our own, we cannot see clearly enough to remove the speck. This picture must have made everyone laugh, but it is true! Specks and planks get in the way and distort our view. Just as sawdust is irritating, we're annoyed by the things we struggle with and we notice them in other people. If I struggle with smoking, for example, I will quickly spot the signs in fellow smokers; I may even feel it is my job to help them, whether they want help or not.

It's so easy for us to label each other and ourselves. We may describe our identity in terms of our job, our church or denomination and our issues, but we are so much more than this.

It does help to admit what we are struggling with. In twelve-step groups, someone may introduce himself this way, "I'm Jack and I'm an alcoholic." In our Christian 12-step group, we encouraged people to say, "I'm Jack, I'm a child of God and I struggle with..."[18] Our identity is not in the speck or the plank. Both Jesus and Paul are inviting us to look past the issue to see the person God created.

Perhaps the "plank" in my eye is the same size as the speck in yours; it may appear bigger only because it's right in front of me. However, our planks are usually out of focus. Try putting your hand an inch or two in front of your eye, then look past it at something several feet away. The hand quickly becomes only a blur, a minor inconvenience. It's easier to focus on someone else's faults, rather than admit my own!

So what do we do about these specks and planks? Jesus does not say we should ignore them. Sawdust specks are painful and harmful to eyes and people may need help to remove them. However, first we have to get rid of our planks. Dealing with one's own stuff is a great leveller and can build into us the humility we need to help others with their issues.

Recognising Planks

I was once driving with my husband, when we came to the outskirts of a small town. Suddenly, I could taste red fizzy pop (not literally, but as if it was real) and memories came flooding back of having been there as a young child. Once a year, our school choir took part in a singing competition. This was the spot where we sat on the coach as teachers handed out cups of fizzy pop before we set off for home.

Our brains are amazing and many things are stored subconsciously or unconsciously. Just being in the same place brought back a taste I had long since forgotten. Sounds, sights, smells and so on can bring up buried memories. If the memories are traumatic, they may surface with intense emotions and we feel as if the event has only just happened.

Judgements can also be buried in the heart, becoming lenses through which we look at the world. They may have been there for so long that we hardly notice them, until our distorted views appear to be truth. They can lead to prejudice, discrimination, and opinions we've held for so long that we've forgotten where they came from.

We could also describe them as bitter root judgements, which we are warned about in Hebrews 12:15, "See to it that no-one misses the grace of God and that no bitter root grows up to cause trouble and defile many."[19]

The writer says we must be careful that they don't spring up and affect other people. Just as plant roots lie dormant in winter, a bitter root can lie dormant for years, yet still have life in it, until one day it springs up and fruit appears. My buried resentments, my prejudices and fixed opinions could "defile" you and "cause trouble" because they may influence the way you see other people.

How do I find these buried roots or planks? If we are willing, God will help us recognise them. Just like weeds in the garden, we really notice them when the leaves and flowers appear, followed by seeds or fruit. What does the fruit of a bitter root look like? Often it will also have a bitter taste, such as a sarcastic comment, an angry outburst or painful emotions that seem to spring up from nowhere. Any overreaction can spring from a hidden root. We might feel confused, ashamed and try to hide our reactions, but they can be clues. If we follow them and discover a root, we can pull it up so that it loses its power!

Removing Planks

I first understood the way judgements work at a training school I once attended. Our small group was asked to select a leader and I secretly hoped I would be chosen, wanting to learn all I could on this course. When another person was selected, I was shocked by the anger that suddenly rose up inside me, which thankfully I managed to keep hidden. This reaction wasn't normal for me and I knew I had to explore what was going on.

I set off on a long walk and God reminded me of my school days when I was in a group of six girls. I was probably number five in the pecking order: if I told a joke, no one laughed, but everyone would fall about if my friend told the same one. My ideas, opinions and suggestions were never listened to, until I felt almost invisible. This kind of interaction between children may seem ordinary and harmless, but it often affects us long-term.

I knew about forgiveness but letting go of judgements was a new key for me. When we forgive, we're looking at what the other person did. Repenting of judgements is taking responsibility for the way I responded. The anger that rose up had been buried, forgotten and hidden away for years in a little pocket of my heart. When it surfaced, I could look at it and then let it go. The key was to repent of the way I had judged my friends and myself, and that's what I did.

A short while later one of the other students knocked on my door. She was on her way to a barbecue and wanted to know if I was coming and bringing my guitar. When the third person did the same thing I had to laugh. God was showing me that something had shifted. It was so unusual for me to be noticed, to be invited or to be recognised in any way. Letting go of judgements is powerful and makes room for blessings. I had judged the friends who didn't see me, judged myself to be invisible, but now that thread was broken.

Removing the Specks

When we understand how this works, we can work with God to help others. Suppose someone behaves towards you in a way that seems rude or offensive. Whether you scold him or accommodate this behaviour, neither approach will help him to mature.

Ask God to help you see him as he really is, to see the potential that God has put within him and try to look beyond the speck. Perhaps he has judged an impatient father and has become like him. Perhaps he expects you to be impatient with him and is defensive. If you confirm his fears he will remain stuck until someone shows him the key to letting go of his bitter judgement.

Many people project their pain onto leaders, because they've judged a father, mother or teacher. If you are the recipient of this, rather than taking it personally, ask God what they need. Empathy is important, but if we give people the key that helps them let go of judgements, they will see more clearly and without so much pain.

Application

If there's something about another person that annoys you, why not ask God to show you if you have a plank in your eye? If you have buried judgements, they could produce weeds in the garden of your heart. They need to be pulled up and put on the fire! They will only cause you trouble and prevent you from seeing clearly.

If you recognise a bitter judgement, try using this prayer:

Father, I recognise that I have judged (name) _____ as (how you described them) _____ .

I forgive _____ .

I repent for my response in judging _____ as _____ .

I ask You to pull up from my heart any stored-up resentment, bitterness or pride and I lay it down at Your Cross.

Please would You release me from my bitter expectation (e.g. "That others will treat me the same way.") _____ .

I lay that at the foot of Your Cross.

Please gather up any fruit that has grown up and affected others and wash them and me clean.

In Jesus Name, Amen.

If I hold on to resentments, they are buried in my heart like seed and I will reap a harvest.

Key 9

What You Sow, You Grow

In this section we are looking at how we mature as believers. We grow stronger when God's Word is alive in us, helping us to overcome the enemy (1 John 2:14). Physical strength comes with good food, exercise and rest; our spiritual food is the Word of God. Some parts are like a delicious meal on a special occasion. Others are like porridge. However, we need both for a balanced diet! We exercise by putting the words into practice. The stronger we become, the more we overcome.

One of the enemy's biggest weapons is discouragement as he brings accusations against us, against others and against God. He tempts us by twisting the truth, whispering lies to get us to doubt God's love. He tested Jesus this way, but Jesus knew the truth. Like Jesus, we can stand our ground when we know what God has said.

If you've never read through the whole Bible, I encourage you to do so. Bible reading plans can help, especially with the more difficult passages.[20] It is full of wisdom and treasure for us to draw on when we need it. You may not like or understand it all, but if you can trust Jesus with your questions, many things will become clearer in time. Reading it will remove any feeling that the Bible is mysterious and unknowable or a deep well you could never fathom.

The Parable Of The Sower

In Matthew 13:19 Jesus compares the Gospel to seed. Seeds of truth are sown into our hearts where, if the soil is good, they develop into healthy plants. As the roots grow stronger and the plants are established, they produce new seeds for us to give away — we want to share the good news with others.

If God's truth can be described as seed, so can the lies of the enemy, who tries to uproot or stifle the new life growing in our hearts. The more we feed on God's Word, the easier it is to identify and discard the lies. Sometimes they look and sound like truth, so we need to know the difference.

I have learned quite a bit about weeds since my first experience as a volunteer. They come in many shapes and varieties and can grow in the worst kinds of soil. Occasionally, you see a beautiful flower, clinging bravely to life in a barren wasteland, but more often these are overtaken by weeds. They may arrive on the wind, be dropped by birds or tunnel below the surface. Some have very little root; others have roots so deep they are extremely difficult to remove. A tiny piece left behind can allow the weed to grow again.

Something else I've discovered is that even good soil has weeds! I used to read this parable and picture the good soil full of healthy plants, with not a weed in sight, but this has not been my experience. Weeds will sneak in or spring up from below the surface when we are not looking! However, if we keep weeding and feeding the soil, the good plants will grow stronger and healthier, leaving less room for weeds to take hold.

When we are tempted to believe lies, we have not failed and should not feel guilty. The enemy whispers lies and then blames us as though we put them there, but really it was him all along. For example, I may be tempted to believe a friend dislikes me, realise I am mistaken, but continue to feel guilty for having such thoughts. If I reject the lie about my friend, I can laugh at this attempt to trip me up (If feelings of guilt persist, forgiving myself in prayer can help me get rid of them.).

These are the weeds that blow in on the wind. We may be offended or irritated, but rather than allowing resentment to grow, we can use forgiveness to uproot it before it takes hold. However, what if this is a pattern in my life, so that I regularly feel this way? There are some lies that have been there for so long, it is difficult for us to distinguish them from truth, and to know how to get rid of them.

Restoration

Our garden allotment is one of several in a large, enclosed field. Sometimes a plot will change hands, as the owner moves away or is unable to continue. Some plots are very healthy. We inherited a beautiful pear tree that gives us abundant fruit every year, but we also gained quite a few nettles and brambles. Plots might be neglected, full of weeds and depleted of nutrients, so the new owners have to work very hard before a good harvest is possible.

When Adam and Eve enjoyed gardening in Eden, there were no weeds: these came after the Fall. The door was opened to death and decay, and all of creation was drawn into the battle for life and health. The natural world reflects our own need for restoration. Thorns and thistles spring up to fill our hearts with confusion, choking us with fear and destroying our relationships.

Through the Cross Jesus restores our connection with the Father and with one another, but we are not free of this world's brokenness. Jesus' death is the ransom, the price paid for our purchase and we now belong to God. However, just like the garden allotment that we bought, we often arrive in a mess! We may put up a sign saying our plot of land has changed hands, but unless we replenish the soil, fill it with healthy plants and keep the weeds at bay, our old ways of thinking and acting will re-establish themselves.

For example, I grew up believing the lie that people in authority are frightening. This "weed" made it difficult for me to relate to anyone in authority. We may learn strategies to cover up such fears, but they often spring up to block or choke healthy connections. Forgiving and letting go of judgements helped me to find the lie and uproot it, but I also needed to plant truth in its place. The truth is that not all people in authority are frightening! How do I plant this seed in my heart, so that it isn't simply something I understand mentally? How do I nurture and protect it until it becomes established and bears fruit in my life? Sometimes it helps to write out a relevant promise or Bible verse and read it aloud every day for several weeks, to help our hearts believe it is true. We also need healthy relationships with people who model God's love and truth to us.

Several years ago, I was introduced to the ministry of John and Paula Sandford. They founded Elijah House on two scriptures: Malachi 4:5-6 and Matthew 17:11. The first states that Elijah will turn the hearts of fathers to their children and children to their fathers and the second, that Elijah will restore all things.

It is interesting that Malachi prophesied four hundred years after Elijah's time, and four hundred years before the second Elijah, John the Baptist. What was it that Malachi, coming in the middle, was highlighting? How does Elijah, or John the Baptist, restore all things? Both challenged people to repent: Malachi explains that our repentance must impact our relationships. In families, he encourages parents to make the first move.

Children need copious amounts of love, affirmation and laughter to become emotionally healthy and resilient. When these are present, the soil in their hearts can more easily resist lies. Where these have been sparse or absent, we need extra nutrients to make the soil healthy. God provides these through our relationships with one another. If we work with Him, recognising and uprooting any weeds that spring up, we will know with a deeper assurance that He loves us.

Follow The Rules

We once visited a YWAM (Youth With A Mission) school in Madagascar, where our friends are missionaries, to teach on healing for the heart. We took along a desk-toy, a Newton's Cradle, which we had bought for our boys from the Science Museum. You probably know how they work, but we wondered if the students, who had never seen one before, would be able to guess. I held up a silver ball at one end and, before letting it go, asked them what they thought would happen next. They had no idea that the opposite ball would bounce, as the middle ones remained still.

The cradle illustrates Newton's theory, that for every action there's an equal and opposite reaction. This is one of the physical laws on which the universe is built, and the same God who designed the world created it with corresponding spiritual laws.

Some of the difficulties we face result from things that happened a long time ago. The cradle's middle balls remain still, representing years of calm, hiding any connection between past and present problems. Like the students, we often have no idea how the two are related. The energy produced by the first ball travels through the middle section, until it explodes into action at the other end. In life we try to manage the bouncing; to control it. We try to get rid of the ball altogether, but only finding the source and bringing the first ball to rest will deal with the reaction.

Paul says, in Galatians 6:7-8, that we reap what we sow: this is both a natural and a spiritual law. Sometimes people assume their bad attitudes are covered by grace, as though that lets them off the hook. When Paul says, in Romans 6:14, that we are not under the law but under grace, he explains that God's law is now written on our hearts; we want to do things His way. Grace gives us the desire and power to change; not an excuse to remain as we are.

How does this law work? If I hold on to resentments, they are buried in my heart like seed and I will reap a harvest. Years later I may have forgotten the original offence, but I know something is wrong. That ball is still bouncing and needs to come to rest; the original hurt and my response to it still need to be resolved. Until this happens, weeds in my heart will stifle the good things that are growing there.

How do I know if I have hidden resentments? James 3:14-16 tells us that bitter envy produces "disorder and every evil practice." We know weeds are alive when the leaves and flowers appear. If we let our resentment go on producing fruit, it will multiply and become stronger. The fruit could be any negative behaviour pattern, overreaction or coping mechanism that I struggle to overcome. This fruit contains more seeds or lies, telling me I'm a failure and making it harder to hold on to truth.

We often respond to negative fruit by trying to manage it. If someone has a drink problem we send them to Alcoholics Anonymous. If there's anxiety, perhaps medication or talking therapy can help. For angry outbursts we suggest an anger management course.

These things can be helpful, even necessary, but what if we could look below the soil and see how those behaviours began? What if they have roots that could be pulled up, so we no longer have to live with them, accept them, hide them from others, or expect people to put up with them? What if they're not really part of who we are?

Here we can be detectives; we ask the Holy Spirit to search our hearts and show us where this began. For example, the person who struggles to feel accepted by friends may recall a time when she was excluded by other children. Now she can use the keys of forgiveness and repentance to bring her resentment to the Cross. This will bring the reaping in her current relationships to rest. She may need to work at building trust for a time, but this will be easier now that the resentment has gone.

The deepest lies are the ones we believe about ourselves. She may believe deep down that she is unloveable. Whatever her mind tells her, her heart believes the lie, but it isn't God's truth. We can bring these lies to Jesus and renounce them, asking Him to plant seeds of truth in their place. There's a prayer below to help you to do this.

When I repent, bringing any resentments and lies (bitter roots) to the Cross, the law of sowing and reaping is satisfied. Jesus reaps in my place so that I no longer have to reap a bitter harvest.

When our Father paid the ransom and bought us back from the enemy, He knew there would be weeding to do. He is not disappointed by this; He invites us to join Him in restoring the garden of our heart. Thankfully we don't have to dig up the whole plot, but as we follow His lead, we discover and uproot weeds, making more room for His love and truth to be established.

In James 3:18 we read that "peacemakers who sow in peace reap a harvest of righteousness."

Application

1. As you read this chapter, were you reminded of any behavioural patterns or coping mechanisms you've been using, without knowing why?

    Are there people who "push your buttons," that you struggle to get on with?

    Do you find it difficult to believe God when He says He loves you?

2. If you answered yes to any of these, take some time to sit quietly with God and ask Him to search your heart and reveal any root.

3. If you recognise a root of unforgiveness or judgement, use the prayers from the previous chapters (7 and 8).

4. If you have believed a lie about yourself, here's a sample prayer to help you bring it to the Cross:

Father God, I've believed a lie that _____ (for example, I am unloveable).

I renounce the lie that _____ .

I repent for believing this lie and come out of agreement with it.

I forgive _____ (name anyone who spoke this over you or who failed to tell you that you are loved) for tempting me to believe this lie.

Please uproot this lie from my heart. I give You permission to put it on Your bonfire and destroy it.

Now ask God for His truth and write down what you hear.

My dear child _____ .

Ask God to show you how to nurture this truth so that it becomes established in your heart.

KINGDOM KEYS

We have not understood our worth, our value to God and how to protect our boundaries.

Key 10
How To Dismantle The Obstacles

There are times in our journey when we seem to hit a brick wall. All of the keys we've used before do not help us to break through. It can be unsettling but we shouldn't be surprised at this. God may be teaching us resilience, perseverance or trust. However, sometimes the wall has been placed there by the enemy, and Father God wants to teach us how to recognise and deal with such obstacles.

We may feel under attack physically, mentally, emotionally or spiritually. Sometimes our finances are affected as resources seem to drain away. There could be many different causes for this. Sometimes these are trials to endure, but some are direct attacks that we can learn to recognise and protect ourselves from.

The Chicken House

Anyone who has kept chickens will know that they need to be protected from foxes. Our chicken house was built to keep foxes and badgers out and so far it has kept them safe. However, every now and then, we discover that a rat has managed to get in and steal the chickens' food. Occasionally, we spot them, helping themselves or scurrying away, but usually we only see the evidence they leave behind: broken eggs, droppings and depleted food. Then we need to find the hole where they gnawed through wood or burrowed under the fence. We patch it up and stay vigilant, waiting for the next time. There will always be rats and we need to be ready for them.

For some of us rats conjure up feelings of fear, even dread (perhaps because of the stories or nursery rhymes they remind us of). In reality, they are more afraid than we are and we can learn to manage them. Some people actually love rats — even the wild ones! However, whether we like them or not, they don't belong with the chickens.

Similarly, in the Kingdom, building safe walls and filling in any gaps or holes can protect us from enemy attacks. John's letter encourages young men who have "overcome the evil one." We've looked at overcoming through repentance, forgiveness, letting go of judgements and rejecting lies. What else might we need to become strong overcomers?

Jesus said in John 10:10 that the thief comes "to steal, kill and destroy." Peter warns (1 Peter 5:8) that our enemy "prowls around like a roaring lion looking for someone to devour." In Matthew 12:44, Jesus uses the analogy of a house to describe a person's life affected by an impure spirit. The spirit may be sent away, but if the "house" remains empty, it will return with more spirits, leaving the person in a worse condition than before. How do we know if such a spirit is present? As with the rats, sometimes we see the evidence that something is wrong, without knowing the cause.

If we ignore the rats that invade our chicken house, like the impure spirits, they would certainly multiply. The chickens would go hungry and they would be put at risk. If we ignore enemy influences, they will always increase and make things worse. How do we make sure our spiritual lives are strong and secure enough to withstand such attacks?

Follow The Instructions

If you've ever built Lego models or flat-pack furniture, you will know that the instructions suggest you begin by checking that you have all the pieces. Some people skip the instructions and that can be disastrous! There may be gaps, pieces in the wrong place, or extra bits added to patch it up, resulting in a model that is out of shape and unstable. If we feel that our life is somehow out of balance, we need to be sure we've read all of God's guidelines. Our character needs to match up with what He says is true, rather than our own ideas of right and wrong.

When Nehemiah returned to Jerusalem from exile in Babylon he found a city in ruins. The walls were broken down, gates had been burned and wild animals could roam the city freely. He began to rebuild the city walls, but this was not without opposition. His enemies tried deception, ridicule, lies, threats and false prophesies, but their intimidation did not succeed. As half of Nehemiah's men built the wall, the other half stood on guard with their weapons.[21]

For many of us this describes the state of our lives when we first come to Christ. Our walls may have been broken down by our sin, or by others' sin against us. We have not understood our worth, our value to God and how to protect our boundaries. We need a strategy for rebuilding the walls, to make it a safe place for our hearts to flourish and thrive. We also need to learn how to recognise the enemy, sometimes a wolf in sheep's clothing, and how to send him away. We need both to build and to be ready to fight.

Safety In Relationships

One area in which our walls may be insecure is in our relationships. When I became a Christian I was so overwhelmed by God's love that I wanted to share it with everyone. I had no idea that my low self-worth was a broken wall that could allow others to break in and steal from me. I had to learn how to protect myself from wolves, and from sheep behaving like wolves. I had to learn how to say, "No," even if that meant disappointing or hurting others. Some people make demands, believing they have the right to be loved, but this is immaturity. Unless we rebuild our walls, and learn to recognise threats, our relationships will be out of balance.[22]

Like Nehemiah's men, we need to do this together. We need a trustworthy community where we can be honest about the things we struggle with, so that we can defend one another as we build.

How often are we really transparent with one another? How many times do we say we are "fine?" A group of us used to joke that "fine" stands for "freaked out, insecure, neurotic and emotional." Then we would ask, "How are you really?" Do you know people with whom you can be totally honest and still feel loved and accepted for who you are? Those are relationships to cherish.

One weapon that we're often encouraged to use is a "word of faith." We may tell someone he can "do all things through Christ," suggesting instant perfection, without explaining that Paul learnt this through years of experience (Philippians 4:12-13). When we find we are not able "to do all things," we might be tempted to put on a mask. We may try to hide our imperfections, failures, negative feelings and all the ways in which we don't look like victorious overcomers, because we feel ashamed.

Of course, faith is important, but some of us have been taught to always be positive and to avoid saying anything negative whatever happens. Imagine how infuriating it would be if your child fell down, broke her leg and refused to admit she was in pain? You would be desperate to help, but locked out, barred by a smile you know is not genuine. How do we let go of this unreality and still express faith in God's power to heal? Our attempts to look good on the outside can block us from receiving what our hearts so desperately need.

In "The Life Model," James Friesen and his co-authors detail levels of maturity that babies and children can accomplish when they are given the right nurture and guidance for each stage of development. When any of these factors are missing, adults remain immature in those areas, even though they are competent in others. Those missing ingredients need to be added or we will remain out of shape and vulnerable; for this we need loving Kingdom relationships. With the right kind of love and encouragement we can learn to trust others and put in healthy boundary walls. We can also help one another recognise places where the enemy has broken in.

The Enemy

Before encountering God's truth, we may have opened our hearts and minds to the enemy. This may have been through curiosity, searching for truth or in response to wounds. If you were raised in a situation where you were powerless or broken, you might look for someone or something to give you protection or strength. When we look in the wrong places we open our lives up to enemy forces who gladly come to "help" us. They bring counterfeit joy, but what promised us peace often turns out to be shackles that trap or bind us, weaving lies that lead us deeper into dark places of fear, confusion or sickness.[23]

When we begin to follow Jesus, as His light comes into our hearts, much of this darkness will flee away, just like the frightened rats. However, sometimes repenting of past sins is not enough to free us from enemy influences. We may still feel drawn to the darkness, or we wonder why God's promises seem to be for others but not for us. Here, we may be dealing with a curse.

Blessings and Curses

In Deuteronomy 28 Moses listed all the ways that God would like to bless us. There are also curses that result from disobedience to God's law. Sometimes I read out the blessings, but once I felt prompted to read out chapter twenty-seven, the list of what brings a curse. The person I was with, who had been experiencing financial difficulties, suddenly remembered she had moved a boundary stone, building a garden wall in the wrong place. I would never have thought of that, but God was showing her why things were not going well. The enemy was taking advantage of this opening. A simple repentance was not sufficient here; only taking action to reverse this mistake would remove the enemy's right to affect this family.

When Paul went to Ephesus (Acts 19), he found a city full of idolatry with a thriving industry for idol makers. When people turned to Christ they burned their idols and occult books along with anything that could influence or entice them back.

Sins that lead to a curse include idolatry, occult practices and shedding innocent blood. This could include past dabbling with Ouija boards, tarot cards, seances and worship of false gods. When we repent of these things God forgives us, but the enemy does not always leave so easily. We also need to renounce the idolatry, to declare that we want nothing more to do with it. It's usually best to do this in prayer with another Christian. This will send away the "wild animals," the forces of darkness that have invaded our land.

If you have opened any doors to darkness, it's a good idea to renounce each form of idolatry specifically, getting rid of any books or objects that connect you to them. If your parents or ancestors opened any doors, you can forgive them and repent on their behalf, standing in the gap for your family.

Addictions

One of the ways we try to ease our pain is through addictions. Any addiction is a form of idolatry that can open doors to the enemy. We go to the addiction for comfort, but never receive what our hearts really need. There are rituals involved as we give homage to unseen forces that try to keep us captive. If we could see the spiritual forces behind the addiction, we might be more eager to renounce our involvement with it.

One common, but often hidden addiction is pornography. When Jesus was teaching about adultery in Matthew 5:27-30, He said that even looking at a woman lustfully is committing adultery in your heart. Pornography is the modern, easy way to look at someone with lust. One practical solution is to block pornography from your computer screens. If this is an issue for you, try to find someone who can help you with this and to whom you can be accountable.

There is forgiveness and cleansing when we repent. If images come into your mind, try bringing them to Jesus. Shame tells us to hide them away, but He already knows they are there. Ask Him to take them and to cleanse and purify your heart and mind.

Repentance may be a journey, but every time you repent from your heart you will strengthen your spirit and your resolve to change and you will weaken the enemy's hold on you.

You may need to forgive whoever first introduced you to pornography. You will also need to renounce this as idolatry. Finding healing for any unmet need can help to restore the broken wall, but you need to actively send away the enemy. If you recognise it is not your friend and can tell the "wild animals" to leave, you will regain authority over your life in this area. It may not be instant, but each time you repent you will strengthen your will and your wall of protection.

Application

If you sense that anything in this chapter applies to you, I encourage you to keep searching until you find answers and the help you need. Learning to receive is hard, but worth it. Some things take time and none of us will find complete healing this side of heaven, but if we can remove any unwelcome "wild animals," things will improve.

The prayer below may help, but for more complex issues we recommend you look for an experienced counsellor, prayer minister or pastor.[24]

A Prayer To Renounce Darkness

1. Father God, I recognise that I have been involved in the sin of _____ . I ask You to forgive me and to wash me clean in Jesus' precious blood.
2. I repent for my involvement in _____ .
3. I receive Your forgiveness and I also forgive myself. I forgive _____ who led me into this sin.
4. I forgive my _____ (father/mother/ancestors) who took part in this sin and I repent on their behalf.
5. I renounce this sin, I want nothing more to do with it, and I ask You to send away any of satan's helpers.
6. Please close any open doors and seal them closed. Amen.

KINGDOM KEYS

CATHY WHEELER

Part 3
Five Keys To The Father's Heart

"I am writing to you, fathers, because you know Him who is from the beginning."
(1 John 2:13)

> **God is always speaking, in many different ways, and He wants us to learn to recognise His voice.**

Key 11
God Is Always Speaking

In this third section, we focus on keys that help us to mature, to become spiritual grown-ups, even fathers and mothers. John says that fathers "know Him." More than accumulated knowledge, they have wisdom flowing from their relationship with Him.

There is a settled confidence in that statement: no striving, no battling, no overcoming; they have found rest in God's unchanging love. A "father in God" is a safe haven because he knows God's heart. To know God's heart we need to hear His voice.

People often tell me that God doesn't speak to them. Sometimes they observe others confidently sharing words or pictures and they conclude they are somehow less important and less gifted. We should always measure our experience against what the Bible says. According to Job 33:14, "God does speak – now one way, now another – though man may not perceive it." God is always speaking, in many different ways, and He wants us to learn to recognise His voice.

We explore some of those ways in this chapter.

Hearing Through God's Word

Firstly, we need to read God's Word, listen to sound teaching and read good books. Sometimes a particular verse or passage appears to jump off the page, as if written just for that moment. We also continually absorb truth until we know things without having to listen for a specific word. We may wrestle for a time with some of what we learn, but once it is settled in our hearts, it becomes part of our treasure. We have heard God's Word, taken it on board and are acting accordingly.

For example, I know it's wrong to steal: I was brought up knowing this. But suppose a person comes into God's family from a background where stealing is acceptable, even encouraged. Before long, this person will be challenged by a pastor, a friend, or his own reading of God's Word. If he agrees with God and renounces this family trait, he will find peace. If not, God will keep talking to him about it, "now one way, now another," until he repents.

Hearing Through Our Conscience

God also speaks to us through our conscience, part of our human spirit. The Holy Spirit brings conviction this way: Spirit to spirit.

Children are born with a sense of justice: they know when things are not fair. They have an inner voice that whispers to them about right and wrong, but this can become dulled over time. When we're born again it is as if a reset button is pressed, and our conscience becomes clean and pure again. However, we may be tempted to ignore that inner voice, cutting corners, taking home "souvenirs" from the office, cheating others because "everyone does it," until that voice diminishes. Peer pressure can dampen our conscience because we don't want to be the odd one out.

Think about the last time you felt a nudge from God to do something. Did you do it? If not, He may be waiting for you to comply before He speaks about the next thing. If we ignore our conscience it gets quieter, until we no longer hear this way. We may need to pray for it to be reawakened by the Holy Spirit.

Hearing Through Creation

Another way God speaks is through His Creation, as described in the following lyrics:

"I can hear Your voice, whispering to me.

Above all the noise, I hear You speak,

Calling me to come, calling me to come.

Rushing through each day, there seems so little time

But I hear You say I need to come aside;

You want to talk with me, You want to talk with me.

I hear You in the mighty wind,

You're whispering through the rustling trees,

And laughing in the bubbling streams,

And weeping in the night.
In the love song of the universe,
The smallest insect's tiny voice,
The anguish of a mother's pain,
The laughter of a child.

I see You in the stars so bright,
And in the eagle's powerful flight,
The closeness of two lovers' arms,
The fragile butterfly;
And in majestic mountains high,
A feather floating gently by;
It's written right across the sky:
You love me, You love me.

But there's so much more You want to tell me,
So much more I need to know,
If only I would listen,
If only I would come,
I'd hear You call me 'friend.'

I can hear Your voice above all the noise

Calling me to come, calling me to come.

He's calling me, He's calling you to come."

The next time you feel moved or delighted by something in creation, why not stop and ask God what it reveals about Him and what He may be saying to you?

Hearing Through My Imagination

God can also speak through our imagination. In his book "Prayers That Heal the Heart" Mark Virkler describes the language of the heart as pictures, music, dreams and imagination. Paul says that our hearts have eyes (Ephesians 1:18). How do we see with our hearts?

Most people can use their imagination to picture something. If I ask a group of people to close their eyes and picture a green sofa, each picture will be different. Or perhaps you can picture the face of someone you love? Sometimes God speaks to us this way, but unless we realise it is God we will say, "Oh, it's just my imagination."

Once, I was with someone who was going through a really difficult time. I suggested we stop and listen to God and then sensed there was an angel next to her, whispering into her ear. It wasn't a clear picture, just a fleeting impression. In the past I may have thought, "this is my imagination," but I've learned to trust these glimpses and to follow the trail they invite me to take.

I asked what she was hearing or seeing. "Nothing," she said. I could have assumed there was nothing, but because I saw the picture, I suggested we listen again. This time I asked different questions. "Is there anything you are sensing? Is God showing you something?" Limiting the question to hearing can lead to an assumption that anything else is irrelevant.

"No," she said, "although a song I was singing yesterday is going through my mind."

I love it when the Holy Spirit leads like this. I sometimes feel like a detective, following clues. The angel was singing to her! When we looked at the words of the song together we found the message God wanted her to hear.

Dreams are similar to pictures, coming through our subconscious mind. Not all are messages from God, but some are. The meaning is often not literal, so think about what the symbols or people mean to you or remind you of. A dog for one person may be a friend and for another, an enemy! It can also be helpful to consider how you were feeling in the dream, as your heart may be trying to inform you of your own buried emotions.

Good Christian books have been written to help you understand the language of dreams, for example, "Healing Dreams" by Russ Parker. If you dream regularly I encourage you to learn more about this; God may be trying to tell you something!

All The Angels Sang

I was once asked to look for a suitable musical for our Junior Church Christmas production. It was August, so I had plenty of time, but I had found nothing so far. We had a very large group that year, with ages ranging from tiny tots to teens. One night when it was very hot and difficult to sleep, I found myself composing a Christmas song. I sensed God's presence, stirring me to listen and tune in to His heart, as I wrote "All the Angels Sang when He was Born."

Next day, I had the crazy idea that I should write a Christmas musical myself. I prayed and quickly wrote Mary's Song. I said to God, "If this is really You, please help me write a song for Joseph." Again, the song came easily, followed by The Wise Men's Song. I remember having fun with that one, as I pictured a dance to go with it.

The musical was a huge success, with all of the children taking part in different ways. They sang, acted, danced, played instruments, worked puppets, moved scenery about, and the church was packed. After our second performance we sent it to a publisher and it is now available from Kevin Mayhew Ltd. This came about all because I recognised that whisper in the night and did not dismiss it as my imagination.

Hearing Through My Mind

Inspiration or wisdom can come as thoughts dropped into our minds. We may sound very wise, but we know we didn't think of them ourselves!

I was once riding into town on a bus when a strange thought came into my head: I am going to be called to do jury service. I dismissed the idea, but a few days later, the invitation came. This was a surprise; it was also concerning because I was due to travel overseas soon after the trial began. Court cases can last for weeks. However, because of my random thought, I decided God was reassuring me that it would be OK. If I was supposed to travel, the case would be over quickly and that is precisely what happened.

Why did God let me know in advance? A pastor friend reminded me that God talks to His friends, and I was becoming a friend. That really touched my heart. We often assume God is testing us, but on this occasion, He let me know so that I wouldn't worry.

Remember Jesus in the boat with the disciples in the storm? He said they were going to go to the other side. When the storm came, it was hard to remember what He had said, until they woke Him up and peace was restored! I wonder what might have happened if they had trusted His words, but then we wouldn't have had the story about the storm being calmed!

Perhaps you can think of a time when you sensed God was saying something and then you doubted? This is not a reason to feel guilty: God is teaching you to recognise His voice. Why not look for His trails and follow them? Who knows where they will lead!

On another occasion, a visiting speaker described a 12-step group that met in his church in America. I had another really odd thought – I would love to go and sing to those people and bless them. Inwardly I took a step back in surprise. Where did that come from? Why would I imagine I had anything to give them?

A few years later, after various steps in a process which involved exploring this 12-step ministry, starting it in our own church, receiving a visit from the leaders and being invited to a conference at their church, the very thing I had imagined actually happened. It was only afterwards that I realised, with amazement, that my "random thought" had materialised! One lady told me it was her first time and the songs I shared really blessed her and gave her the courage to keep going to the group. God does speak to His friends, so ask Him how He speaks to you. When something drops into your spirit, don't dismiss it but explore it with Him, or with a friend.

Hearing Through My Emotions

Sometimes we recognise things are not as they appear. A friend may be smiling but we sense he is actually sad, angry or fearful. Communication takes place on many levels, and rather than dismiss these feelings we can ask God what to do with them. He may want us to pray for the person or to reach out in some way.

Sometimes we sense God's emotions. We may feel tremendous sadness or anger at injustice. We may sense His joy when His love is shared. We know a family who have cared for a boy with special needs since he was a baby. Now in his twenties, he loves the sound of people worshipping. When people pray with him he often begins to giggle. He clearly senses the Father's joy and this delight quickly spreads to everyone around. He is nonverbal and his understanding is limited, but he recognises the Father's love!

Hearing Through Others

God may speak to us through a word of encouragement or prophecy. There are a few things to consider here.

Paul encourages us all to "eagerly desire … the gift of prophecy" (1 Corinthians 14:1). This is a gift we give to one another, imparting strength, encouragement and comfort.

Words that give direction, correction or a promise should normally be given by someone with experience and need to be weighed or tested. We should also ask God for confirmation.

If we receive a promise, God expects us to work with Him, rather than to sit back and wait for it to be fulfilled. For example, if someone suggests you are called to the mission field, you may need to do some research and training first.

Some people begin, "God says…" or "Thus saith the Lord…" appearing to give the words more authority. A better phrase would be, "I sense that God may be saying…" This may help you, the hearer, realise you can disagree if you believe the word is incorrect.

Be careful not to put the speaker on a pedestal. The Holy Spirit gives gifts of faith, wisdom, discernment and so on. He is all-seeing and all-knowing, but the person speaking is not.

And remember, even well-known prophetic voices get it wrong sometimes!

Prophetic words should be taken "with a pinch of salt." By this I mean a covenant of salt, a relationship with someone you might eat a meal with. Ask the opinion of your family, your pastor, your leader. Of course, if these people are unsafe, you may need confirmation from elsewhere.

If you are receiving a personal prophecy, make sure you have laid down any strong desire to hear a specific promise or direction and you are willing to hear whatever God has for you. The person praying may confuse what comes from your soul with God's voice; you may hear the words you hoped for, but this will not help you.

If you go to a meeting where words are being given, lay down any desire you have to receive this way. It can be tempting to feel left out or unseen, but God can speak to you in different ways.

I was once in a meeting where I really didn't want or expect to be given a word, and that is when the most important one came.

In the next chapter we will look at ways we can improve our ability to hear God's voice.

Application

1. How does God speak to you?

2. Think about a time when something in creation moved you. What did it show you about God, the Creator? What might He have been saying to you?

3. Have you received a prophetic word? Take some time to ponder what was said and ask God to show you if there is more He wants to say.

Why not journal about these things?

KINGDOM KEYS

CATHY WHEELER

How do we recognise God's voice?

Key 12
Our Hearts Have Ears

If God is always speaking, why is it sometimes so hard to hear Him?

Did you know that your heart has ears? In 1 Kings 3:9, Solomon asks for a "discerning heart," literally a "hearing" heart.[25] Just as our hearts have eyes, they have ears, but hearts can become deaf.

Most of us can hear with our physical ears. Our minds interpret and understand what we hear, but the heart is where we store our treasure. The things we know, believe and value in the depths of our hearts steer our lives, even when we are unaware of their influence. Many of us have learned so well how to operate out of reason, we've forgotten how to listen with our hearts — the wellspring of our lives (Proverbs 4:23).

Have you been in conversations where everyone appears to be listening, responding and arguing literally, yet missing what others are trying to say? These sometimes become heated confrontations, where only one person wins. Have you also experienced being heard even when your words were jumbled or inadequate? Or have you been able to hear past the words to what others are trying to say? This is listening with the heart.

Jesus said, John 10:27, "My sheep listen to My voice; I know them and they follow Me." The sheep of Jesus' day were not chased and herded by dogs and whistles, they followed shepherds who called each one by name. As we continue to follow our Shepherd, our hearts learn to hear and recognise His voice. We listen because we know it is Him.

How do we recognise God's voice? If we are not used to hearing Him, where do we begin? Firstly, we should expect Him to speak, and listen for His voice. Ask Him a question and look out for the answer — it may come in an unexpected way.

God doesn't always use words; He sometimes speaks to me through birds! He might catch my attention with a singing blackbird or thrush, then drop some truth into my spirit. Once I was asking if I should attend a particular conference and He replied with a group of goldfinches. This was the first time I'd seen them in our garden; my heart was delighted and I took it as a sign of God's favour.

We don't have to be weird about this. He speaks to us individually in a way we can hear, but always we test this against what His Word has already revealed.

Make Time To Listen

It's good to intentionally spend time in God's presence, just as you would take time to meet with a friend.

I wrote the following song in response to a talk by Barry Kissell. I often use this to help me draw aside and reconnect with God.

"I will still my heart

In the quiet place.

You call me to the desert

You draw me to the wilderness.

I will still my soul

As I wait for You,

I will resist the darkness,

I will fix my eyes on You.

I long to hear Your voice,

To know Your presence in my heart.

I need Your healing touch;

Speak to me, Lord, of Your love.

And I will wait, I will wait,

Until You come;

And I will wait, I will wait for You,

I'm waiting."

At times we struggle to hear God's voice, even if it was once much clearer. We may stumble into a desert place because of our own choices, but sometimes God leads us there. If you feel that God has disappeared, or withdrawn, He may be drawing you to a place of deeper intimacy with Him, leaving the shallows for deeper water. This is not a place to splash around but to be still.

I "will" still my heart. These words remind me to intentionally stop and listen. God is always speaking; I need to tune in to His voice. How do I still my heart when I am troubled? By bringing all my concerns, all the people on my heart, and placing them in His hands, so I can focus on Him and listen.

Verse two invites me to still my soul. My mind and emotions may be restless, so I use a notepad. As I write down any distracting thoughts, lists and so on, they come out of my head onto the pad, and I can concentrate on listening.

There will be opposition so don't be surprised if you have to battle to take this time, or to keep your thoughts pure or fixed on Him. If you are tempted, remember that temptation is not sin. Rather than wrestling with the thoughts, turn your thoughts and the eyes of your heart to Jesus and focus on Him.

Verse three reminds us that He lives in us and that our spirits long to be with Him; to hear Him. This may sometimes get drowned out by other voices, but it is what you were made for. Allow that longing to grow, to rise up in you. Pour out your heart to God and listen for His response. In this time of waiting we honour Him, as our hearts learn to hear and see His love.

Listening Through Meditation

Some people avoid meditation because the word has become associated with other religions and New Age practices, which involve emptying the mind. Christian meditation is very different, and can be described as pondering or chewing something over. Rather than beginning with an empty mind, we take a verse, passage or topic and spend time getting more from it.

There are various ways to do this but I will share my approach.

- I choose about six Bible verses and ask God what He wants me to know about this passage.

- I read it through once or twice, taking note of how it impacts me, and any questions it raises.

- Then I read it aloud a few times, putting the emphasis on different words each time. Sometimes I personalise it, using "I" instead of "he," "they" and so on.

- I might ask Jesus, "Why did You say that?"

- I try to picture being there, to imagine His face, especially His eyes. Often, instead of the serious Jesus I had heard someone preach about, He reveals to me a twinkle in His eye when He said those things.

I find that Jesus becomes more real to me this way, and His words make more sense.

You could also meditate on a word, an aspect of God's nature, a character and so on.

Listening Through Soaking

Soaking is another way to connect with God. This usually involves prayerfully resting and listening to instrumental worship music. I first experienced soaking after a friend recommended trying it with a Ruth Fazal CD. Ruth is a Christian violinist, songwriter and singer who writes beautiful worship and orchestral music that can lead you into God's presence. Of course, other CDs are available!

I had been at a leaders' meeting where someone had prayed for me, and then said, "Do not hasten from the presence of the Lord." I sensed this was a prompt to try soaking. A few days later, when everyone was out, I put the new CD on and lay on the sofa. What followed was amazing.

With my eyes closed, I pictured a little girl and I sensed she was me. I was on a mountain top, like Julie Andrews in "The Sound of Music." Then followed a series of pictures, like a movie that took me through my life thus far. In one scene after another I recognised myself, my heart, but now I was looking from a different perspective, seeing it from God's viewpoint. It took me through some dark times, and I saw that, even though I had felt completely alone, He was there, bringing me through to a place of hope.

This was a deeply healing time for me; God was continuing the healing He began at the meeting. I recommend soaking as a way to recuperate, recover and take in any new thing God is doing in your life, especially after receiving healing prayer.

Soaking can help us tune in to God's heart. We may hear something specific, for ourselves or others, or we simply rest in His presence. You may want to begin with a Bible verse, but it is good to have no agenda.

If you find you become distracted, keep a notebook handy to write down any interrupting thoughts.

Listening Prayer

All prayer should be listening prayer — making room for God to speak to us. However, there is a type of listening prayer we sometimes use in ministry sessions, especially with anyone who finds it difficult to connect with his own heart. If someone asks, "How did you feel when that happened?" and you struggle to remember, trying harder only makes it more difficult. Instead, we ask Jesus, because He knows. I may ask, "Jesus, how did John feel when this happened?" Now that John is listening to Jesus, the pressure to come up with something is gone, and we often hear an answer this way. Learning to connect with God spirit to Spirit is very similar to listening with our hearts.

Listening By Stepping Back

Sometimes, in the middle of an emotionally charged meeting or discussion, it's difficult to know what to say, how to respond, how to be. Afterwards we may think of something we could have said or done differently, but it's too late.

If you are a person who easily empathises with others, sensing what they're feeling and soaking up atmospheres, negative or positive — this can be painful. If you are aware of others' pain or embarrassment you might speak up vehemently, realising later that in your passion you overstepped the mark. Or the pain may block you, even cripple you and leave you unable to interject anything.

How should we manage this?

I find it helpful to consciously take a step back from these situations into my spirit. It is rather like Lucy in the wardrobe, suddenly surrounded by other people's coats that were pressing in on her, blocking her view, and pushing her backwards. She stepped back right out of the wardrobe into another world and landed in the snow!

We can take a step back into Jesus, because He is always with us. In that moment, with practice, we learn to sense whether to be quiet or to speak.

How should we do this? Rather like a radio, we need to flip the switch and tune in to a different channel. Our heads may be engaged in the argument or whatever turmoil is going on around us, but our spirits can still tune in to God's Spirit. An arrow prayer, a silent "Jesus, help!" can be useful. If you pray in tongues you could do so silently, and this can help you to hear Him more clearly. Sometimes you can literally go into a different space for a few moments so that you can hear your own heart and God's voice more clearly. Depending on the circumstances, a visit to the bathroom or kitchen, or going outside for some fresh air, can give you enough space to stop and hear God.

When we learn to step back into our spirits, just like Lucy in the snow, we find that everything is quieter. The argument may still be raging, but we have stepped into a place of rest. This is where maturity is.

Just like a parent who knows when to interject and when to be silent, we can learn to hear Father God's wisdom and it is always better than our own.

When I was a new believer I was so shy that I hardly ever said anything. At times I sensed God was nudging me to speak, and I would be silently praying before opening my mouth. People got the impression that I was very wise, because I only ever said the things He asked me to. If I had shared all of my thoughts they would have realised this was far from true!

Today, I often pray silently in my spirit language when there is conflict and this helps me to hear God's voice more clearly. It can also help to silently put the Cross of Jesus between you and the others in the room, so that their stuff doesn't affect you so much. We're not responsible for other people's decisions, outbursts or maturity. God may be working in ways I am not aware of. If I try to jump in and fix the situation, or rescue people, I may be getting in the way of what He is doing rather than helping!

Listening For Others

It can be very intimidating to be put on the spot and asked to come up with a word or prayer for the person next to you. I remember finding that really difficult, convinced I would get it wrong. However, when you dare to take that risk and find that the other person is grateful, encouraged and blessed by what you share, you realise this is a gift we can all learn to give one another.

This is something you could practise, hopefully with a safe group of friends. Even the so-called experts had to start somewhere. If you get a fleeting impression you could share it and say, "I don't know if this means anything to you but..."

It may be that a particular verse of scripture or a song pops into your mind. It might be something God showed you recently.

Grab for the fleeting idea before it escapes and share that, rather than trying hard for something to come that sounds "better." We don't need to sound like anyone else. The more we learn how God speaks, take time to meditate, soak and listen, the more natural it will be for us to hear God's heart for others.

I was once praying with a man who struggled to trust that God was there for him. Each session, whenever I asked him to picture Jesus, he saw a lion (like Aslan in the Narnia books). Before our last session I was reminded of one of the Narnia stories about Eustace, and I began by sharing this with him. That morning I had also sent a prayer request to our team, giving no details of the sessions, in the hope of a breakthrough with him. Usually

I would turn off my phone but I left it on just in case a reply came through. A text message came referencing another Eustace story, and I shared this with the client.

He was amazed and asked if we always talk about Narnia in our meetings. I assured him that we didn't. This was God, speaking loud and clear: "I am here for you and will help you." Finally, he was able to give his fears to God and receive what he needed from Him.

Our friend had no idea of the impact her impression about Eustace would have. Sometimes what you share is just a small part of the puzzle, but it may be the piece that unlocks the place where someone else is stuck!

Application

1. Take some time to sit with God and use the song lyrics above. Go through the stages outlined in each verse. Use a notebook to write down any impressions you have about what God is saying to you.

2. Choose a passage from the Bible and use the meditation ideas detailed above. Write down any thoughts, insights, questions and revelations.

3. Find some instrumental worship music and spend some time "soaking" in God's presence. Begin with prayer and ask Him to speak to your heart. Relax and don't try too hard but go with the flow.

4. Try journalling. Write a letter to God, telling Him what is in your heart. Then write "God says…" followed by anything you sense He may be saying to you in reply.

KINGDOM KEYS

If I ask you who you are, how would you answer?

Key 13
Becoming Who You Are

Just after my seventeenth birthday I went on an Outward Bound Course. This was a four-week course at a centre in Wales, for girls aged 16-21. The course offered a variety of activities designed to be stretching and character-building. Our headmistress encouraged all six-formers to go, and of the three of us that went that year, none was particularly sporty or out-going.

I felt like a fish out of water. Here I was with all these strangers, mostly older than me, attempting various kinds of physically demanding challenges. On the second expedition our group leader sprained her ankle, and we all gathered round the trainer to find out who would take her place. No one was more surprised than I was when she picked me! I'd never led anything or anyone before. Did she see something in me no one else had noticed? I was usually at the back, trying to encourage a girl who was always grumbling, complaining and slow. I had to step forward and somehow all the stronger characters rallied round in support!

The scariest part for me wasn't the abseiling, high ropes, canoeing, caving and so on, but the three short talks we had to give to our groups. I was painfully shy and hated having to read aloud in class. Hardly anyone would hear me and if the teacher complained, I'd get even quieter. During an earlier adventure centre visit, I was even given the nickname "O silent One." Despite all this, somehow my third talk went so well, everyone was talking about it at breakfast the next morning!

We can easily disqualify ourselves if we look only at the outside. When we put ourselves and others in boxes, we don't see the gifts God has placed within us. Did I return home, more confident and outgoing? Well, not exactly: I still found it tremendously difficult to speak in public or to imagine that I could be a leader. Today I do have opportunities to teach and lead and I love being in that role. Slowly I've been discovering who I am.

Recognising The Obstacles

Some of the biggest obstacles we face on this journey are those we've put in place ourselves. As a young child I decided I would be quiet; it was a way to protect myself from the chaos around me. We call these decisions unspoken inner vows.[26] At the time, this served me well. In my somewhat dysfunctional family it was often safer to observe and keep quiet. I also soaked up a lot of emotional weight from those around me, with no way of expressing how I felt. A great deal was locked inside of me in an unhealthy way.

Since then I have gradually been able to unpack what was never mine to carry and to find my voice. I have discovered that I do have something worth saying.

Many of us have made similar unspoken inner vows, often as children, to protect our hearts from being wounded. Here are some examples:

I would never do that/say that.

I will never trust anyone again.

I will always be a good girl/a good boy.

As children they can help us, but as adults we need to let them go. The safety barrier they provide becomes a prison, preventing us from becoming who we really are. However, we are often unaware of their existence until we bump into them! If you are wrestling with inner conflict, if you would love to try something but feel blocked or afraid or if you sense a battle between your head and your heart, ask God if there is an inner vow at work.

Children often make vows to protect themselves or their families when they feel insecure. A great example of this can be seen in the Disney film "Inside Out" in which a little girl decides to be happy all the time, hiding her feelings of sadness from her family. This does not go well and she begins to shut down emotionally, until her family's love helps her to find herself again. I often recommend this film to people who come for ministry — it's not just for children!

Vows can lock away parts of our personality that need to be rediscovered and set free. There are vows to hide and vows made in a desperate cry for acceptance. Perfectionism, for example, is not a personality trait but an unhealthy response to insecurity, fear or pride. Aiming for excellence is good, but if we are driven to perform for approval, we have not yet discovered our identity.

Growing Good Fruit

If I ask you who you are and you reply that you are a new creation in Christ, that your identity is in Him — this is only part of the answer. This describes your position as a child of God, living in His Kingdom, but not your individual character. A parent with several children, who loves each one equally, will be able to tell you how varied, special and delightful their individual personalities and giftings are. The God who creates every snowflake different does not make cookie-cutter Christians!

God wants us all to become more like Jesus, but every person who reflects His character will be different, because none of us could begin to exhibit the fullness of His amazing love and goodness.

Your identity is also not in your gift or your job. Some churches emphasise the importance of gifts and roles. However, the role is not who you are; it's what you do. God gives gifts to bless and strengthen the church, not to give us self-worth. Whatever our gifts, the real test of maturity is our character. Am I becoming more like Jesus in the way I serve others?

How Do I Find Out Who I Am?

Books and courses that identify personality types can be of some use. It can be a relief to discover that being a quiet, gentle introvert is just as good as being more outgoing and an extrovert, especially if others have pushed you to be more assertive. However, if I had assumed that being painfully shy and withdrawn is my identity, I may never have found my voice.

I once prayed with a lady qualified to help people discover their personality type. She was so convinced of her own analysis, she was unwilling to consider that a certain behaviour pattern might need addressing. She viewed it as part of her identity, rather than a reaction to difficult circumstances. Her refusal was keeping her from becoming who she was made to be.

Understanding our differences can be helpful. I know I am more of an introvert who benefits from time alone to refocus and refuel, whereas my husband benefits from interaction with other people. However, this is different from putting each other into boxes, failing to look for the potential for change.

Growing Up Into Christ

God's intention is for healthy families to surround each child with unconditional love, so the child can rest in his or her identity and live from a place of security. The parents help him find out who he is. What gifts has God placed in this child? What are his strengths? What does he enjoy?

I used to say that our third son was a mixture of his two older brothers, until I asked God one day to reveal his unique gifts and identity. A few days later he announced that his favourite subject at school was physics. Physics! That was my least favourite, and we are not sure who he gets this from! I might have dismissed this as a passing fad, but I believed this was God's response to my prayer so I encouraged his interest. He doesn't need to become a great physicist. We can enjoy discovering the things our children delight in and encourage them to try new things. Sadly, our education system tends to funnel children through a system of academic success or failure, so that only a few discover fulfilment and achieve their potential.

Some parents, who perhaps were not allowed to become the musician, scientist or sportsman they longed to be, will urge their children to do the thing they missed out on. If the child has the same passion, this encouragement and support will help him to succeed. If not, it will be a painful struggle, as he wrestles between pleasing his parents and following his own heart.

We probably all know people who are not sure who they are. We can ask God to reveal His plan. If someone is like a square peg in a round hole, help her find a square hole, don't demand that she become more round!

When unconditional love has been lacking, present day relationships can fill in the gaps as we try to discover who we are. This is what Paul describes in Ephesians 4:15. Rather than putting one another in boxes and closing the lid, we can help one another "in all things to grow up into ... Christ." There is a process of maturing that comes through safe, loving relationships.

Love Or Demand?

However, the walls we've built to protect our hearts as children can make it difficult for us to receive the love we need. We may struggle to recognise love when it comes in forms we are not used to. We may have made inner vows not to need love, or only to receive a certain kind of love.

Imagine only being willing to open the cube-shaped gifts under the Christmas tree. Think how many delightful presents you may be missing out on! If we can learn to recognise love in all its varied wrappings, our hearts can be met and filled with love that comes in different ways, helping us to mature.

This can take time and we need to be patient with ourselves and each other. However, the Holy Spirit is our Teacher; He will lead us one step at a time. Rather than demand that love come only in a certain shape or colour of wrapping, why not ask Him to help you take down those walls, so that His love can touch your heart in a new way?

Growing Through Adversity

Most of us would prefer not to encounter obstacles. Rather than seeing them as opportunities for growth, we often look around for someone to blame. Is it my fault, your fault or an enemy attack? If I can convince myself it was not supposed to happen, I can remain passive: a victim of someone else's bad choices. However, James says we should be joyful when we encounter all kinds of problems, because these are opportunities for us to mature (James 1:2-4).

Some things are sent, or at least allowed by God, to test us. When rope is tested it is stretched. New car models are tested by being crashed a few times! Did you know that gold is tested by being heated up until a person's face can be seen reflected in it? God tests us so that we reflect more and more of His character. He tests you, not to find out what is in you – He already knows! He wants you to realise what should not be there and then to work with Him in removing it, repairing it, or replacing it with His treasures.

This doesn't mean that God is responsible for all the difficulties in our lives. Sometimes we find out why things happen, as God equips us to fight our enemies. Some mysteries will remain, but God promises He will be with us, working for good in all circumstances. If we look for Him, He will show us the next step to take.

Tracing The Rainbow

When I was at school I told the careers teacher I would like to become a teacher. She laughed. I don't blame her. My voice was so quiet, no one would have heard me.

Today I do teach, although not in schools. My first step in this journey was as a songwriter. Someone once called my songs "heart songs." I like that. They are written from my heart, expressing what is in my heart, helping others express theirs and revealing God's heart for us. I have realised they are also teaching songs, as I try to share the things God has shown me.

Perhaps you can look back over your life and recognise different colours, shades and patterns pointing to the person you are becoming? We can't undo the past, but as we look back with God we often discover that He was there all along, singing His love song over us and inviting us to join in. Even before we knew Him, and especially at those times when we thought we took the wrong path, He was there, preparing the way for us to find His love and our lives in Him.

Application

1. If I ask you who you are, how would you answer? In the light of what you've read, does your answer need to be re-evaluated?

2. Do you find it easy/difficult to receive love? Why do you think this is?

3. Ask God to show you if you have made a vow not to need love, or to limit the ways love can be shown to you.

4. Ask God to show you any other inner vows you made to protect your heart, especially in childhood.

5. Use the prayer below to let go of any vow you recognise.

Prayer:

Father God, I renounce the vow that I made, that I will (never/always) _____ .

I place this vow on the Cross, and ask You to set me free from its prison walls.

I declare that You are my Protector, and I choose to find my security in You.

Please help me to recognise love in all its forms and give me wisdom as I learn who to trust, and how to give and receive safe love.

Please help me to become the person You created me to be.

Amen.

> *The trials and wounds you have experienced can become your strengths, like a thread of gold woven through your life.*

Key 14
Are We There Yet?

We've been discussing identity: becoming the person God made us to be. Here we look more closely at how we mature as believers. Just as we train and prune plants to produce more fruit, the obstacles we face can help us to grow as God guides us through them. They can be opportunities for our perseverance and brotherly kindness to increase (see James 1:2-4; 2 Peter 1:5-7).

In Matthew 7:15-19 Jesus says you can tell a true prophet from a false one by the fruit he produces. What did He mean by fruit? Some point to the number of people they've led to the Lord, to programmes or buildings, but Paul's description of fruit in Galatians 5:22-23 is all about character.

Of the nine qualities Paul mentions – love, joy, peace, patience, kindness, goodness, faithfulness, gentleness, self-control – which do you find the most easy or difficult in your relationships with other people? It would be great if we could focus on our favourites, but God wants all of them to be growing in our lives! What are some of the ways in which God prunes us so that these qualities increase?

I Write To You ... Children

As a new Christian I was lent a cassette tape of teaching by an American pastor. I don't remember his name, but his message impacted me deeply. He was speaking on 1 John 2:12-14 — my framework for this book. Here is my recollection of what he said, plus a few thoughts of my own:

John is writing to people, not according to their physical ages, but their maturity as believers. As "children" we need to know we're forgiven and that the Father loves us. When we grasp this truth, we have a strong foundation on which healthy growth can begin. We might picture small children at the seaside, splashing about in ankle-deep water; full of joy and hope.

"Are we there yet?" Parents or carers will recognise this question, especially on long journeys! What children really need to know is that they are secure, they belong and someone else knows the way.

When we first enter the Kingdom, we have not yet arrived: this is just the beginning. New Christians often grow very quickly. A secure baby learns how to show patience and kindness by imitating those who love him. A young Christian in a safe, loving environment can also produce strong, healthy fruit from the beginning. He will be full of faith and joy, eager to learn and grow. With older and wiser Christians to guide him, he will be ready for the next steps in the journey.

I Write To You ... Young Men

John writes that as we mature, we understand more of God's Word and His ways. We know we are in a battle, learning to recognise and overcome different kinds of temptation, enemy attacks such as discouragement or shame and the deceptive lure of sin. Here we can picture a person standing in deeper water, perhaps waist-deep. This signifies a cleansing and purifying of ungodly passions and desires. It takes more effort to walk through the water or to swim.

For teenagers, things can become very bumpy for a while as they attempt to figure out life for themselves. Tensions can arise as they navigate their way from dependence to independence. Wise parents, secure in their own identity, will give them room to explore and make mistakes, remaining ready to help them make course corrections or to welcome them back with open arms.

We understand that this is a normal (if tricky) step on the way to adulthood, and it is rarely easy. Have we understood that the journey to maturity as Christians is similar?

In the Kingdom, there's a battle to fight and we need to play our part. C.S. Lewis illustrates this in "The Lion, The Witch and the Wardrobe" when Peter refuses to use a sword. He holds on firmly to his childhood values, that is, until his sisters are in danger. Then he discovers within himself a strength he didn't know was there, defending them from their attacker and, from that moment, becoming a skilful warrior.

As we stay connected to the Holy Spirit we find a new depth to the love and peace in our hearts. The river that Jesus promised springs up from within, producing better, purer fruit. We realise, for example, that kindness is not the same as being nice; it can be kinder to tell the truth, even if it hurts. We learn to respond from renewed hearts, discovering a deeper, more courageous love for others.

In the third book of "The Chronicles of Narnia" series, "Prince Caspian," Peter and his brother realise that righteous passion, when mixed with pride, can become destructive. In "The Silver Chair" Lewis also describes how the enemy attempts to disarm us through deception.

As young believers grow stronger, some things become more difficult. The river of life brings to the surface old ways of seeing and responding. If we struggle to be patient, for example, trying harder will not work. Just as the children in Narnia had to face and overcome their childish responses, dealing with the source of our impatience will make room for the fruit of patience to develop.

If we do not understand that obstacles are normal, if we believe we should already be "there," mature and complete, then what do we do when we fail? The temptation is to pretend everything is fine, to wear masks and to deny to ourselves and others that there is a problem. In doing so we also deny ourselves the opportunity to grow through the problem.

At this stage Christians, like teens, can become over-confident, critical or discouraged. They may focus on their victories and revelations without understanding that there is so much more to learn. They may become disillusioned when they realise the people they looked up to are also not yet perfect; they may give up trying when what has been promised seems to take too long. If there is no one to help them handle this immaturity or to deal with their discouragement, they may withdraw, leave or set off down a path of extremism.

We have such a great need for fathers and mothers who are willing to share their wisdom and experience. Then the enthusiasm of the young can be held within arms big enough to overlook minor confusion and offences, but strong enough to lovingly challenge and correct error.

I Write To You ... Fathers

Let's look at what John wrote about this third group, "fathers and mothers in God."

John mentions the first two groups twice, varying his words each time to build the picture. For fathers, he uses the same phrase both times: "You have known Him who is from the beginning." This gives both the statement and the stage it describes a sense of completeness; there is nothing more to add.

Fathers have gone through the battle and have come to a place of rest. Now the water is too deep to stand up in and the person is carried. He is not swimming frantically; he rests in the certainty of God's unchanging nature and faithfulness. The water washes over his chest, as his heart is fully God's. He knows, not only that he is forgiven and how to fight; he knows the Father's heart.

At the end of his talk, the pastor made an appeal for anyone willing to become a father or mother in Christ. He said there is a huge lack because so few are ready to make this commitment. Spiritual maturity, unlike physical growth, doesn't just happen. We have to be intentional, willing to tackle the hard stuff and push through the obstacles.

Growing Up In Christ

Is John suggesting that we should all become fathers and mothers in God? Is this the goal of our discipleship?

In this sense, yes: John describes a father in God as one who knows the Father, who knows His heart. This is a picture of maturity that we can all aim for. Whenever we encounter a difficult situation, we can ask God where He is, and what He wants us to know. He promises we will find Him when we search with all of our hearts (Jeremiah 29:13).

When I first heard this message, even though I was still a baby Christian, I said yes to God. I have never regretted doing so. Something changes inside when we respond to God's call. People began to come for advice and prayer; perhaps they would have come anyway, but I expected God to hear us and answer our prayers.

I did not suddenly become an "adult"; I still had a long way to go! We don't have to wait to be fathers and mothers before we begin sharing what God has given us. When we all give what we have, however small, we make room in our hearts for more of His love.

In Ephesians 4:13-16, Paul explains that we grow best when everyone is involved. They say it takes a village to raise a child, and the same is true when it comes to restoring the broken and wounded people who come into God's family. This does not negate the need for expert help and experienced counsellors, but we all have a part to play.

Maturity is not measured by how long we have believed, how much of the Bible we know, our role, gifts or experience. It's measured by how much more like Jesus we are becoming and for this we need relationships.

"Then we will no longer be infants... speaking the truth in love we will in all things grow up into Him who is the Head, that is Christ. From Him the whole body... grows and builds itself up in love, as each part does its work" (Ephesians 4:14-16).

I recommend finding a group of believers with whom you can learn, grow and serve. You don't have to be an expert. Love will do its work if we are willing to give to and receive from each other.

I remember once sharing something from my past with two friends. They were not counsellors, but they were good listeners. Later, I became quite anxious, wondering whether I had made the mistake of sharing too much. I was afraid it might affect our relationship; they might treat me differently. The next time I saw them I was greeted with the usual, "Hi Cathy," with no hint of awkwardness. It was such a healing moment! I had already prayed through these things with a counsellor, but to be welcomed and accepted by "family" can be even more healing.

What Is A Father Or Mother In God?

You can recognise them.

They are the people that feel safe, that you are certain will be able to tell you how God feels about something you haven't been able to find an answer for.

They are the ones who have wisdom and will answer your question – even if it's just a line in an email in response to an outpouring of your heart that was several pages long – and you know at once that they have asked God what to say. They haven't just replied out of their own head or experience because it hits you in your heart and feeds you with His love.

They are the ones that help you to hold on and trust even when you feel as if you are sinking. They are able to be an anchor without drowning themselves because they know how to keep giving you to God and not become overwhelmed by the responsibility or weight of your pain, even while being able to empathise with you and make you feel heard.

They know how to set boundaries when you cannot; they will gently but firmly keep them in place without sending you away.

They won't allow you to put them on a pedestal, even though for a time they may let you lean on them, until you have enough strength to transfer your trust to Jesus and other safe people.

Do you know any one like this? Are you willing to become this person for someone else?

The trials and wounds you have experienced can become your strengths, like a thread of gold woven through your life. If you are willing to do the hard work of forgiveness, repentance, letting go of your defence mechanisms, fortress walls, disappointments, judgements and disillusionment, and if you allow God to fill the deserts with springs, then you will take back land stolen by the enemy. You will build bridges for others to cross so they won't have to go to the depths you went to. They can learn from you and go further than you. This is the mark of a parent, helping his offspring to stand on his shoulders and achieve more than he did.

These are all pictures of what happens in the heart when we cooperate with God in this process.

Application

1. Which of the three stages do you most relate to: child, young person or parent in God?

2. Ask God if He is calling you to become a mother or a father in Christ?

    If so, what is your response? Why not talk to Him in about it in prayer?

3. Are you in a group in which you can share your heart, your struggles, your triumphs? If not, ask God to lead you to a group where you can grow.

4. Read 2 Peter 1:5-7. Here is a list of the qualities Peter mentions:

    Faith, goodness, knowledge, self-control, perseverance, godliness, brotherly kindness, love. Pick one of these and ask God how you can strengthen this quality in your walk with Him.

5. Ask God if there is someone to whom you can show something of the Father's heart.

KINGDOM KEYS

> *The hero is always Jesus.*

Key 15
What Is In Your Bag?

A few years ago, during a team meeting in which we were prayerfully listening to God as "soaking" music was playing, I saw the following picture. It provided the seed from which ideas for this book first began to grow and take shape.

The Treasure Chest

I was offered a beautiful chest which I was invited to open. Inside it were several ornate, shiny keys, of different sizes and shapes. Among the golden and silver ones I noticed one key that was small, dull and brown. I sensed that I was supposed to choose a key, and that it should be this small one. I took it out and looked around for somewhere to use it.

I could see a small door at the side of the road I was standing on. The door, brown and wooden, was almost hidden by the long grass that grew above it and all along the road. It reminded me of a Hobbit's house! I went over and tried the key in the lock. It fitted, so I turned it and opened the door.

There was a deep darkness inside which was almost tangible. As my eyes grew accustomed to this I could just make out a person, far back in the room. I sensed there was something evil around this person.

The door was far too small for me to go inside and I wondered how I could help. I began to speak, and as my words flowed into the room it was as if they turned into golden musical notes. I was speaking truth, and I sensed that this went on for a long time, far longer than the actual time that passed as I watched this scene unfold. Gradually, little by little, the words brought light into the room, and the person inside was slowly revealed, so that I could see her face. The evil around her did not like the light, so the thick darkness began to withdraw deeper into the depths of the room.

Finally the girl, who had been trapped in this place, had enough strength to come towards the door and take my hand. I was able to pull her through into the daylight. As she emerged and blinked she caught sight of her family, who had appeared behind me. She ran past me into their arms and they embraced.

This was for me a profound picture of the work of prayer ministers and others who help to set people free, bringing healing and reconciliation to families and other relationships.

Now my job was done, but as I looked along the road, feeling very drained, I noticed that many more little doors had suddenly become visible. I sensed God was asking me, "Will you continue this work?" I felt humbled, because I know that it is only His grace and power that sets the captives free, but He chooses to partner with us if we are willing. And so I said, "Yes, I will continue."

I don't believe I was the hero in this picture; the hero is always Jesus and His words of truth, which pushed back the darkness and set the prisoner free. And the hero is the girl, who had the courage to wait for help, to take my hand and to step out from that dark place into life and freedom.

I was the willing servant; watching Jesus set people free is a hugely rewarding privilege. However, there are many more doors that need unlocking and many more prisoners to set free.

As you read this description, did you find yourself identifying with anyone in the picture? Perhaps the girl, trapped in the darkness? Perhaps the person with the key? Or perhaps you see yourself as part of the family, welcoming those who have been set free and are in need of family love so that they can recover and grow strong?

We are not all called to be pastors, counsellors or prayer ministers, but if you do sense this call on your life, then accountability and being part of a team is really important. Some of the deepest wounds have occurred when a person has risked trusting a father or mother figure, only for that trust to be betrayed. When this happens in churches, the impact can be devastating. We need to be sure we are caring for our own hearts so we do not end up hurting others.

Where Are The Fathers?

My friends at Elijah House describe a father or mother in God as a person who can love others to life. Here are the lyrics of a song I wrote after spending time with them.

"She used to wonder how it felt

To hold a father's hand;

She'd watch the children laugh and play:

She couldn't understand

How they could run into their father's arms,

And never seem afraid,

And she knew something was missing deep inside.

Like a foreign language,

That she had never learned,

She didn't know when it was safe to trust,

Or when to be on guard.

But she was hoping for someone

To tell her who she was,

'Cause she knew something was missing deep inside.

Where are the fathers who can love her to life?

Where are the mothers who will hold her in their hearts?

So many broken who need to understand

The Father's heart of love for His children.

And she knows that she can't live again

All the years lost and gone,

But if someone could relieve the pain,

Then she could learn to trust again.

The Father sent her someone

Who understands His ways,

Who taught her how to follow Him,

To listen and obey.

Now she can run into her Father's arms,

And never feel afraid,

'Cause she's found out what was missing deep inside.

Where are the fathers...?"

Parable Of The Talents

In Matthew 25 Jesus tells the Parable of the Talents, where the servant with one talent chooses to bury it rather than use it to make more. The master is angry and throws him out, taking even the one talent away from him.

This story used to scare me and I was not sure I liked the Jesus that would throw people out because they were afraid. However, parables give us only part of the picture and we need to look deeper for the meaning, measuring what we find against other truths revealed in the Bible.

This parable shows us that everyone is given something valuable. Some have more talents, but no one is worthless or without some special gift with which he can bless others. We do not earn it; He made us that way.

Secondly, any gifts I have do not belong to me. Even so, if I begin to use my gift for the Kingdom, there will be joy and fulfilment for me as well as blessings for others. Again, He has made us this way.

Many years ago a man came to me and said he believed I was burying the talents God had given me. I think his aim was to encourage me, but he was not aware of the baggage I was carrying, nor the lies I had believed that were holding me captive in a prison of hopelessness. Rather than encouragement, his words added to my feelings of shame, despair and my desire to hide.

We may see potential in others, but we cannot assume their pathway ahead will be straight and without obstacles. Most of us need help to get free of the shackles of the past as we grow from the old into the new. Just as Lazarus emerged alive but bound from the tomb, we need one another's help to change our old ways of thinking, believing and behaving.

I have been the girl trapped in the little house of darkness. I have experienced truth being whispered, sung and spoken over me by others willing to serve God in this way, until finally I was able to step into a place of freedom and begin to heal.

As we find freedom, we receive keys from others who have gone that way before us, and now we have treasure that we can share.

A Box Of Keys

What do you have in your bag that you could share with others? Do you hold keys that could help others who are stuck as you once were? We often limit ourselves, believing that others will do a better job. We may believe we have to reach a certain standard before we can begin to bless others.

If you can offer a smile and words of encouragement, you may be feeding a brother or sister with hope. If many voices are singing at the door, perhaps those trapped inside will be able to step out of prison more quickly.

Application

1. Which keys in this book were challenging for you? Why not read that chapter again and work through the steps in prayer. You could also look for more books on that subject.

2. In the treasure box picture, which person or group do you most identify with? What do you need to help you to grow?

3. If you sense a calling to minister to others, is there someone with experience you can share this with? I encourage you to get some training so that you can learn how to do this safely and effectively.

KINGDOM KEYS

CATHY WHEELER

Endnotes

1. Psalm 22:9

2. See Luke 12:32; Matthew 18:3

3. Jeremiah 29:11

4. Blaise Pascal (1623-1662) wrote of an "infinite abyss" that could be filled only by God Himself who is "infinite and immutable."

5. Netbible.org Psalm 84 Note 13

6. See Hebrews 12:7-12; James 1:2-12

7. "Sub" or "shub" (Hebrew) is similar to "tubo" (Aramaic). Although John's words were recorded in Greek, he and Jesus probably spoke Aramaic. "Sub" or "tubo" expresses what John was teaching.

8. Hebrew Greek Keyword Study Bible

9. We are body, soul and spirit. The soul is often described as the mind, will and emotions. The human spirit is often synonymous with the heart, or inner being.

10. Hebrew Greek Keyword Study Bible

11. I first heard Mark Sandford teaching on the "Heart and Mind" at an Elijah House training school.

12. "Nacham" usually refers to God relenting out of compassion, for example, "If that nation I warned repents (sub)... then I will relent (nacham)" (Jeremiah 18:8). "Out of His great love He relented" (Psalm 106:45).

13. Romans 2:4

14. Matthew 3:11, "He will baptise you with the Holy Spirit and with fire."

15. Hebrew Greek Keyword Study Bible

16. Paul's letters are written in Greek, but he was a highly educated Jew who understood Hebrew, and most likely also spoke Aramaic.

17. Paul echoes Jesus' teaching in Romans 2:1.

18. Celebrate Recovery

19. For more on this, see "Transforming The Inner Man" by John and Paula Sandford.

20. "Daily Bread" and "Encounter with God" are available from Scripture Union (scriptureunion.org.uk). I also recommend Nicky Gumbel's "The Bible in One Year" available in book form and from the YouVersion Bible App. Eden.co.uk is an online bookstore carrying several guides of varying depth to studying the Bible, eg. by Tom Wright (aka NT Wright).

21. Nehemiah 4:16

22. John Townsend and Henry Cloud have written a very insightful book on this subject called "Boundaries."

23. Books such as "The Bondage Breaker" by Neil Anderson explain this in more detail.

24. Ministries that offer appointments include Elijah House, Freedom in Christ and Sozo.

25. Hebrew "sama" means to hear, listen, obey; be heard.

26. For more on this see "Growing Pains" by John and Paula Sandford.

CATHY WHEELER

Recommended Reading

Loved Like Never Before

Ken Symington

The Orphan Heart

Steve Hepden

The Life Model

E. James Wilder, James Friesen, Anne M. Bierling, Maribeth Poole, Rick Koepcke

Transforming The Inner Man

John Loren and Paula Sandford

Growing Pains

John Loren and Paula Sandford

Grace And Forgiveness

John and Carol Arnott

Prayers That Heal The Heart

Mark Virkler

Boundaries

John Townsend and Henry Cloud

Bondage Breaker

Neil Anderson

Blessing Or Curse: You Can Choose

Derek Prince

Addicts and Those Who Love Them

Robert and Kathie Fetveit (free course available from heretohelpintl.org)

Healing Dreams

Russ Parker

Turning the Hearts of Fathers

Mark Sandford

KINGDOM KEYS

CATHY WHEELER

About The Author

Cathy Wheeler is the founder of Hearts Resounding Ministries, a ministry that seeks to bring personal transformation to individuals through inner healing, and to equip people to share this healing with others. She trained in prayer ministry with Elijah House USA and Austria, learning principles of transformation taught by John and Paula Sandford. She is a Facilitator of EH training schools in UK. Besides teaching in the schools, she has spoken in conferences and church services. Cathy has a Masters Diploma in Ministry from the Wagner Leadership Institute.

Cathy has also served as a worship leader and has written and recorded several songs, including a children's musical.

She is married to Phil and they have three adult sons.

CATHY WHEELER

Other Books

All The Angels Sang

A Christmas Musical For Children

Published by Kevin Mayhew Publishers

Something different here! A musical of the Nativity story for "human" characters and Muppet-style puppets, building up to a joyful finale: a party scene complete with balloons and party poppers! There's plenty of scope for singing (some solo), dancing and acting, or working "behind the scenes," changing backdrops and scenery. The detailed production notes give helpful advice on stage layout and how to make and use the backdrops. There's even a step-by-step choreography of the fun "Wise Men's Walk."

CATHY WHEELER

About PublishU

PublishU is transforming the world of publishing.

PublishU has developed a new and unique approach to publishing books, offering a three-step guided journey to becoming a globally published author!

We enable hundreds of people a year to write their book within 100-days, publish their book in 100-days and launch their book over 100-days to impact tens of thousands of people worldwide.

The journey is transformative, one author said,
"I never thought I would be able to write a book, let alone in 100 days... now I'm asking myself what else have I told myself that can't be done that actually can?'"

To find out more visit
www.PublishU.com

CATHY WHEELER

Printed in Great Britain
by Amazon